TU TRAVEL GUIDE

2025

The Essential Turin: Explore History, Culture, and Cuisine.

BY

ZERA CANTRELL

Copyright © 2024 ZERA CANTRELL.

All Rights Reserved.

Table of Contents

Disclaimer 5

Introduction 9

    Why Turin?: Discovering Italy's Hidden Gem 12

    A City of Elegance and History: The Allure of Turin 16

    How to Use This Guide: Making the Most of Your Visit ... 19

Chapter 1: Getting to Know Turin 23

    A Brief History of Turin: From Roman Times to the Modern Era 23

    Turin at a Glance: Neighborhoods, Culture, and Local Life 26

    Best Times to Visit: Seasons, Festivals, and Events 30

Chapter 2: Exploring Turin's Historic Heart 35

    Piazza Castello & The Royal Palace: The Heart of Turin's Grandeur 35

    Mole Antonelliana & National Cinema Museum: Icons of Italian Cinema and Culture 38

    Via Roma & Piazza San Carlo: Strolling through Turin's Elegant Shopping Streets 41

Chapter 3: Art and Culture in Turin 45

Museo Egizio: The World's Finest Egyptian Collection
Outside Egypt...45

Galleria Sabauda: Masterpieces of the Savoy Dynasty.....50

Contemporary Art Scene: Where to Find Modern
Creativity..55

Chapter 4: Savoring Turin's Culinary Delights 61

Piazza Vittorio Veneto's Cafés: Sip Espresso Like a Local 61

Eataly Turin: A Gastronomic Journey in One Place.........65

Chocolate Heaven: Gianduiotto and the Birthplace of
Nutella..70

Chapter 5: Hidden Gems and Local Favorites 75

The Balon Market: Vintage Finds and Antiques Galore ...75

Borgo Medievale: A Step Back in Time Along the Po River
....79

Quadrilatero Romano: Where History and Nightlife
Collide 83

Chapter 6: Day Trips from Turin 89

The Royal Residences of Piedmont: Palazzos and Gardens
Fit for Royalty 89

Sacra di San Michele: The Stunning Abbey on the
Mountaintop 95

Barolo and Langhe Wine Regions: Sipping the World's Finest Wines 100

Chapter 7: Practical Information..107

Getting Around Turin: Public Transport, Walking Routes, and Bike Rentals 107

Where to Stay: Accommodation for Every Budget 113

Insider Tips and Safety Advice: Navigating Turin Like a Pro 119

Conclusion... 125

Disclaimer

This travel guide is designed to provide accurate and up-to-date information about Turin to help enhance your travel experience. While every effort has been made to ensure the accuracy and reliability of the content, the rapidly changing nature of travel and local conditions means that some information may become outdated or subject to change. The author and publisher are not liable for any errors or omissions, or for any consequences that may arise from the use of this guide.

Regarding Images:

Please note that this guide does not include images of Turin or its attractions. This decision was made to focus solely on delivering rich, detailed descriptions and practical information that can assist you in planning and enjoying your visit. Here are the key reasons for this approach:

Focus on Detailed Descriptions: By prioritizing comprehensive descriptions and practical advice, we aim to provide you with a thorough understanding of Turin's attractions, neighborhoods, and experiences. Our goal is to immerse you in the essence of the city through words, allowing you to visualize and appreciate Turin in your own way.

Dynamic Nature of Travel: The appearance of landmarks, streets, and attractions can change over time due to renovations, new developments, or seasonal variations. Including images may not always reflect the most current state of these places, potentially leading to discrepancies between what is seen in the images and what is experienced in reality.

Encouraging Exploration: We believe that part of the joy of travel lies in personal discovery. By relying on detailed descriptions rather than images, we encourage you to engage with Turin directly and uncover its beauty and charm through your own exploration.

Practicality and Accessibility: A text-only format ensures that the guide remains accessible and easy to navigate without the need for additional digital resources or downloads. This approach helps in keeping the content focused and practical for all readers.

We appreciate your understanding and hope that the detailed insights and tips provided in this guide will enhance your experience of Turin. Should you require visual references, numerous online resources and travel websites offer up-to-date images and additional visual context to complement the information in this book.

Safe travels and enjoy your journey through Turin!

Introduction

Welcome to Turin, a city where elegance meets innovation, where rich history mingles effortlessly with contemporary flair. Often overshadowed by Italy's more famous cities like Rome, Florence, and Venice, Turin is an undiscovered gem that offers travelers a unique blend of regal architecture, world-class museums, cutting-edge art, and culinary delights that are second to none.

Nestled in the shadow of the Alps and cradled by the Po River, Turin is the former capital of the Kingdom of Italy and remains a city steeped in grandeur and tradition. From its stately boulevards lined with Baroque palaces to its vibrant piazzas buzzing with café culture, this northern Italian treasure is a destination that rewards the curious traveler who seeks authenticity away from the crowded tourist paths.

Turin offers the perfect mix of old and new. Marvel at the intricate architecture of the Royal Palace and stroll under the elegant porticos that stretch for miles across the city. Dive into the world of Italian cinema at the Mole Antonelliana and lose yourself in the fascinating collections of the Museo Egizio, one of the finest Egyptian museums in the world. And when it's time to refuel, Turin's historic cafés invite you to indulge in decadent chocolates, aromatic coffee, and the birthplace of the iconic gianduiotto.

Yet, Turin is more than just historical landmarks and culinary delights. It's a city with a contemporary soul. Vibrant neighborhoods like the Quadrilatero Romano come alive at night with trendy bars and eateries, while cutting-edge art galleries and creative spaces pepper the city, showcasing Turin's thriving arts scene.

This travel guide is designed to be your trusted companion as you explore everything Turin has to offer. Whether you're here for a weekend getaway or an extended stay, we've crafted this guide with the curious traveler in mind. Inside, you'll find insider tips, local favorites, and practical advice to help you make the most of your visit. Each chapter takes you deeper into Turin's neighborhoods, cultural treasures, culinary experiences, and hidden gems. You'll learn not only where to go, but also why each place is worth your time.

We've also included detailed maps, transportation tips, and day trip suggestions to ensure your journey is seamless from start to finish. Whether you're an art lover, a history buff, a foodie, or simply a curious explorer, this guide will help you uncover the true essence of Turin.

Get ready to experience a city that's refined yet unpretentious, historic yet forward-thinking—a place that invites you to explore its layers, savor its flavors, and make lasting memories. Welcome to Turin, a city where tradition meets innovation and every corner tells a story.

Why Turin?: Discovering Italy's Hidden Gem

A City of Regal Grandeur

As the first capital of unified Italy, Turin still exudes an air of regal charm. Strolling through its tree-lined boulevards and grand piazzas, you can feel the echoes of its royal past. The city is adorned with opulent palaces, such as the Royal Palace of Turin (Palazzo Reale), located in Piazza Castello. A UNESCO World Heritage Site, this palace was once home to the powerful House of Savoy and showcases stunning interiors, including the dazzling Hall of the Throne. Nearby, the Palazzo Madama—a former fortress turned Baroque masterpiece—adds another layer of historical richness to Turin's cityscape.

What sets Turin apart is its distinctive atmosphere. The elegant porticoes that line streets like Via Roma offer not only shelter from the weather but also a leisurely path for window shopping or enjoying a classic bicerin (a traditional drink made of coffee, chocolate, and cream) at one of the city's historic cafés like Caffè Al Bicerin (Piazza della Consolata 5).

Cultural Treasures and Artistic Delights

Turin's culture is a blend of the classical and the contemporary. The Mole Antonelliana, with its iconic spire, is home to the National Cinema Museum (Museo Nazionale del Cinema), a must-visit for film enthusiasts. The museum's interactive displays and panoramic elevator ride to the top offer an immersive experience unlike any other in Italy. For history buffs, the Museo Egizio (Via Accademia delle Scienze 6), one of the largest collections of Egyptian antiquities outside Cairo, is a treasure trove that leaves a lasting impression.

Turin's love for the arts also extends to its vibrant contemporary scene. In the Quadrilatero Romano, the city's ancient Roman quarter, you'll find quirky galleries and independent art spaces. Streets like Via della Consolata and Via San Domenico come alive with exhibits and events during Artissima, Turin's annual contemporary art fair.

Gastronomy: The Heart of Turin's Identity

No visit to Turin is complete without indulging in its renowned culinary scene. The city is famous for its aperitivo culture, where evenings start with a glass of vermouth—which was invented here—paired with an array of small bites. Head to Baratti & Milano (Piazza Castello 29), a historic café dating back to 1858, for a taste of Turin's refined confections.

Turin is also a haven for chocolate lovers. The city is the birthplace of gianduiotto, a smooth, hazelnut-infused chocolate that's still crafted with care at artisanal shops like Guido Gobino (Via Lagrange 1). Don't miss a visit to Eataly (Via Nizza 230), where you can explore the best of Piedmontese cuisine, from truffles to fine wines.

Turin's Green and Scenic Spaces

Despite its urban elegance, Turin offers abundant green spaces and riverside promenades. Parco del Valentino, located along the Po River, is the perfect place for a leisurely walk or a picnic. The park's Borgo Medievale, a 19th-century recreation of a medieval village, adds a whimsical touch, making it a delightful stop for families.

For those looking to venture further, the city is the gateway to the stunning Piedmont countryside, where you can explore the renowned wine regions of Barolo and Langhe or visit the breathtaking Sacra di San Michele, a clifftop abbey that inspired The Name of the Rose.

A Hidden Gem Worth Discovering

Turin's allure lies in its ability to seamlessly blend its grand historical legacy with a dynamic, forward-thinking vibe. It's a city where you can step back in time within grand palaces, sip a coffee in a café frequented by intellectuals, and discover cutting-edge art all in one afternoon. Whether you're drawn by its history, its culture, or simply the chance to experience a more authentic slice of Italy, Turin is a hidden gem that promises unforgettable memories.

A City of Elegance and History: The Allure of Turin

The Royal Grandeur

At the heart of Turin's allure lies its royal past. The city's status as the first capital of unified Italy (from 1861 to 1865) has left it with a legacy of grandeur that is still palpable today. Begin your exploration at Piazza Castello, the grand square that serves as the epicenter of Turin's historical splendor. Dominated by the Royal Palace of Turin (Palazzo Reale, Piazza Castello, 10122 Torino), this magnificent Baroque edifice was once the residence of the House of Savoy. The palace's opulent interiors, adorned with gilded decor and stunning frescoes, offer a glimpse into the lives of Italian royalty. Don't miss the Armory Museum within the palace, which houses an impressive collection of weapons and armor.

A short stroll from Piazza Castello, the Mole Antonelliana (Via Montebello, 20, 10124 Torino) stands as one of Turin's most iconic landmarks. Originally conceived as a synagogue, it now hosts the National Museum of Cinema. The Mole's unique architecture and panoramic observation deck provide sweeping views of the city and the surrounding Alps—a perfect spot for photography enthusiasts.

Cultural Corners

Turin's cultural scene is equally compelling. The Museo Egizio (Via della Consolata, 5, 10122 Torino) is renowned for its unparalleled collection of Egyptian artifacts, making it a must-visit for history buffs. With over 30,000 items, including mummies, statues, and hieroglyphs, this museum offers an immersive journey into ancient Egypt.

For art aficionados, the Galleria Sabauda (Via XX Settembre, 3, 10122 Torino) is a treasure trove of masterpieces from the Renaissance to the Baroque periods. The gallery's extensive collection includes works by notable artists such as Caravaggio and Rubens, providing a rich tapestry of Italy's artistic heritage.

The Essence of Turin: Gastronomy and Cafés

No visit to Turin would be complete without indulging in its culinary delights. Piazza Vittorio Veneto is a vibrant hub where locals and tourists alike gather in its numerous cafés and bistros. Caffè San Carlo (Piazza San Carlo, 156, 10121 Torino) is an institution, offering a classic Italian café experience. Here, you can savor a rich espresso or an exquisite hot chocolate, a nod to Turin's status as the birthplace of gianduiotto, a creamy hazelnut chocolate.

For a more contemporary dining experience, Eataly Turin (Piazza Solferino, 1, 10121 Torino) is a must-visit. This sprawling gastronomic complex combines restaurants, markets, and specialty shops, all under one roof. It's the perfect place to sample local delicacies, from truffle-infused dishes to artisanal cheeses and wines.

Hidden Gems

Turin is full of hidden gems that offer a deeper understanding of its local life. Borgo Medievale (Viale Virgilio, 107, 10126 Torino) is a reconstructed medieval village that offers a charming escape from the city's modernity. Located along the Po River, this area features quaint streets, a castle, and beautiful gardens that provide a picturesque setting for leisurely walks.

Another local favorite is The Balon Market (Piazza della Repubblica, 10122 Torino), an antiques and flea market that takes place every Saturday. This vibrant market is a treasure trove of vintage finds, ranging from antique furniture to retro clothing and collectibles.

How to Use This Guide: Making the Most of Your Visit

1. Understanding the Layout

Our guide is structured to offer a comprehensive view of Turin, divided into sections that cover the city's main attractions, local experiences, and practical advice. Each chapter is designed to help you explore a different aspect of the city:

Getting to Know Turin: Start here to get a feel for the city's layout, its history, and the best times to visit. This section helps you understand the context of what you're seeing and provides a foundational knowledge of Turin's neighborhoods and landmarks.

Exploring Turin's Historic Heart: Dive into the must-see historical and cultural sites, including iconic landmarks and essential attractions. This section is ideal for first-time visitors wanting to experience the essence of Turin.

Art and Culture: For art enthusiasts and culture seekers, this chapter highlights the city's rich artistic heritage and contemporary cultural scene. Discover world-class museums and art galleries that showcase Turin's artistic prowess.

Savoring Turin's Culinary Delights: Turin is renowned for its gastronomy, so this section will guide you through the best places to sample local specialties, from traditional dishes to modern culinary creations.

Hidden Gems and Local Favorites: Explore Turin beyond the tourist trail with recommendations for local markets, quirky neighborhoods, and lesser-known attractions.

Day Trips from Turin: If you have time for excursions, this chapter provides suggestions for nearby destinations that offer additional cultural and natural experiences.

Practical Information: Finally, this section includes practical advice on getting around, where to stay, and essential tips for a smooth visit.

2. Planning Your Itinerary

Use the detailed descriptions in each section to plan your daily itinerary. For example, if you're passionate about art, dedicate a day to visiting the Museo Egizio (Via Accademia delle Scienze, 6) and the Galleria Sabauda (Via XX Settembre, 86). Allocate another day to exploring the culinary scene, starting with a breakfast at Caffè Torino (Piazza San Carlo, 204) and ending with a dinner at Eataly (Piazza Solferino, 1).

Consider using the day trip recommendations for extended stays. For instance, a visit to the Sacra di San Michele (Via Sacra di San Michele, 1) is easily manageable in a day and provides a stunning view of the Piedmont countryside.

3. Local Tips and Recommendations

Look out for local tips sprinkled throughout the guide. These include insider advice on the best times to visit popular attractions to avoid crowds, local eateries where you can experience authentic cuisine, and practical suggestions for navigating the city's public transport system.

For example, if you're interested in experiencing Turin's vibrant café culture, the guide suggests visiting Caffè Platti (Via Roma, 37), which is renowned for its historic ambiance and traditional pastries. Similarly, to truly enjoy the local nightlife, the guide recommends the Quadrilatero Romano district, where you'll find lively bars and charming eateries.

4. Maps and Transportation

Detailed maps are provided to help you orient yourself within the city. The guide also offers practical advice on public transportation options, including trams, buses, and the metro. For instance, the Torino Metro (line 1) connects key areas of interest and is a convenient way to travel.

If you prefer walking, the guide includes suggested walking routes that take you through the city's most picturesque streets and neighborhoods. For longer distances or day trips, consider renting a bike or using a local taxi service.

5. Customizing Your Experience

Finally, feel free to customize your visit based on your interests. Whether you're a history buff, an art lover, a foodie, or someone who enjoys hidden gems, use this guide as a flexible tool to craft a memorable experience tailored to your preferences.

Chapter 1: Getting to Know Turin

A Brief History of Turin: From Roman Times to the Modern Era

Roman Beginnings

Turin's history dates back to Roman times, when it was known as Augusta Taurinorum. Founded in 28 BC, this settlement was strategically positioned along the major Roman roads that connected the Po Valley with the rest of the empire. The city was named after the local Celtic tribe, the Taurini, who inhabited the area before Roman colonization.

One of the most significant remnants of Roman Turin is the Porta Palatina (Piazza Cesare Beccaria, 10122 Torino), a well-preserved city gate that once formed part of the Roman city walls. This impressive structure, built in the 1st century AD, offers a glimpse into Turin's Roman past and serves as a notable landmark in the city today.

The Medieval Period

During the medieval period, Turin grew in prominence as a commercial and political center. By the 11th century, it was part of the powerful Savoyard domain. The Savoy family played a crucial role in the city's development and its eventual rise as the capital of the Kingdom of Sardinia in 1720.

One of the most iconic medieval sites in Turin is the Basilica di Superga (Piazza Superga, 10132 Torino), perched on a hill overlooking the city. Built in 1731, this Baroque masterpiece is not only an architectural gem but also the final resting place of many members of the House of Savoy. The basilica offers panoramic views of the city and the Alps, making it a popular spot for both its historical significance and scenic beauty.

Renaissance and Baroque Flourishes

The 17th and 18th centuries saw Turin transformed into a showcase of Baroque architecture and urban planning. The city's architectural evolution was largely driven by the Savoy dynasty, which sought to enhance its prestige and influence.

The Palazzo Reale (Piazza Castello, 10122 Torino), or Royal Palace, is a prime example of the city's Baroque splendor. Originally a medieval fortress, it was expanded and renovated during the 16th and 17th centuries to become the grand residence of the Savoy kings. Today, it houses a museum with exquisite furnishings and royal artifacts.

The Birth of Modern Turin

The 19th century was a period of significant change for Turin. In 1861, the city became the first capital of unified Italy, marking a pivotal moment in Italian history. Turin's role as the political and cultural heart of the new nation was solidified during this era, as it became a hub for industrialization and modernization.

One notable figure from this period is Giuseppe Garibaldi, the Italian military leader who played a key role in the unification of Italy. His legacy is honored with a prominent statue in Piazza Carignano (Piazza Carignano, 10121 Torino), a central square that also features the historic Palazzo Carignano. This building, designed by the architect Guarino Guarini, served as the seat of the first Italian Parliament.

Contemporary Turin

Today, Turin is known for its dynamic blend of historical charm and modern innovation. The city's industrial past, particularly its association with Fiat, has evolved into a focus on technology, design, and culture. Turin's transformation is reflected in its vibrant arts scene, world-class museums, and revitalized public spaces.

The Mole Antonelliana (Via Montebello, 20, 10124 Torino), originally conceived as a synagogue, now stands as a symbol of Turin's resilience and modernity. Home to the National Museum of Cinema, it represents the city's rich cinematic heritage and its ongoing role in shaping the future.

Turin at a Glance: Neighborhoods, Culture, and Local Life

Neighborhoods to Explore

1. Centro Storico (Historic Center)

At the heart of Turin lies the Centro Storico, a captivating area where the city's rich history is on full display. Begin your exploration at Piazza Castello, the city's central square, surrounded by grand buildings like the Royal Palace of Turin (Piazza Castello, 10123 Torino). The palace, once the residence of the House of Savoy, offers a glimpse into royal life with its opulent rooms and lush gardens. From Piazza Castello, stroll down Via Roma, known for its elegant arcades and high-end boutiques. This street leads to Piazza San Carlo, often called the "Salotto di Torino" (Turin's living room), where you can relax in one of the historic cafés like Caffè San Carlo (Piazza San Carlo, 10121 Torino).

2. Quadrilatero Romano

For a taste of Turin's vibrant nightlife and culinary scene, head to the Quadrilatero Romano, an area teeming with trendy bars, restaurants, and street life. The cobblestone streets and historic buildings provide a charming backdrop for modern social spots. Visit the bustling Balon Market (Piazza della Repubblica, 10122 Torino), a sprawling market offering antiques, vintage goods, and a lively atmosphere. In the evening, enjoy dinner at one of the local trattorias, such as La Casa del Polpo (Via del Carmine, 18, 10122 Torino), known for its fresh seafood and traditional Piedmontese dishes.

3. Vanchiglia

Just across the Po River from the Centro Storico, Vanchiglia is a bohemian neighborhood that has become a hotspot for Turin's artistic community. The area is home to the beautiful Murazzi del Po (Lungopo del Po, 10100 Torino), a series of arches along the riverbanks now used for art exhibitions and cultural events. Visit the Fondazione Merz (Via Limone, 24, 10141 Torino), a contemporary art space housed in a former factory, showcasing cutting-edge art from both Italian and international artists. Vanchiglia's narrow streets are lined with quirky shops and cozy cafés, making it a perfect area to explore on foot.

4. San Salvario

Known for its eclectic mix of cultures and vibrant nightlife, San Salvario is one of Turin's most diverse neighborhoods. The area is renowned for its multicultural flair and a variety of international cuisines. For a unique dining experience, try Ristorante Da Cianci (Via del Carmine, 19, 10122 Torino), which offers traditional dishes from various regions of Italy. San Salvario is also home to the Porta Palazzo Market (Piazza della Repubblica, 10122 Torino), one of the largest open-air markets in Europe, where you can find everything from fresh produce to local crafts.

Cultural Highlights

Museo Egizio (Egyptian Museum)

Located at Via Accademia delle Scienze, 6, 10123 Torino, the Museo Egizio is one of the most important Egyptian museums outside Egypt. With an extensive collection of artifacts, including mummies, statues, and papyri, it offers a fascinating insight into ancient Egyptian civilization.

Mole Antonelliana and National Cinema Museum

An iconic symbol of Turin, the Mole Antonelliana (Via Montebello, 20, 10124 Torino) houses the National Cinema Museum. The building itself, originally intended as a synagogue, offers panoramic views of the city from its observation deck and features interactive exhibits on the history of film.

Galleria Sabauda

For art lovers, the Galleria Sabauda (Via XX Settembre, 3, 10121 Torino) is a must-visit. This gallery showcases an impressive collection of Renaissance and Baroque paintings, including works by masters such as Van Dyck and Rubens.

Local Life

Turin's local life is a blend of traditional Italian charm and modern vibrancy. The city is known for its café culture, with historic cafés like Caffè Torino (Piazza San Carlo, 204, 10121 Torino) serving as gathering spots for both locals and visitors. The local markets, from the bustling Porta Palazzo to the antique stalls at Balon, reflect the city's rich cultural diversity and offer an authentic shopping experience.

Best Times to Visit: Seasons, Festivals, and Events

Spring (March to May)

Spring is one of the most delightful times to visit Turin. The city begins to bloom, and the weather is pleasantly mild. Daytime temperatures range from 10°C to 20°C (50°F to 68°F), making it ideal for exploring the city's many outdoor attractions and parks. The crisp, fresh air adds a touch of magic to your walks through the historic center or along the Po River.

Key Events:

Salone del Libro (Turin International Book Fair): Held annually in mid-May at the Torino Esposizioni (Corso Massimo d'Azeglio, 15, 10126 Torino), this is Italy's largest book fair. It attracts authors, publishers, and literary enthusiasts from around the world, offering book signings, panels, and readings.

Festa della Primavera: Celebrated in late March, this festival welcomes the arrival of spring with street performances, markets, and food stalls in the Piazza Vittorio Veneto, a lively square known for its stunning views of the river.

Summer (June to August)

Summer in Turin is warm, with temperatures often exceeding 30°C (86°F). This is the perfect time to explore Turin's open-air activities and enjoy its many outdoor cafés and terraces. The city comes alive with a vibrant atmosphere, and numerous festivals fill the calendar.

Key Events:

Torino Jazz Festival: Typically held in late June, this festival features a series of concerts in various venues throughout the city, including the prestigious Teatro Regio (Piazza Castello, 215, 10124 Torino). It's a must-visit for jazz enthusiasts.

Estate Reale: This series of summer concerts and cultural events takes place in the historic gardens of the Royal Palace (Piazza Castello, 10122 Torino). The events usually start in July and offer a blend of classical music, opera, and theatrical performances.

Autumn (September to November)

Autumn is a wonderful time to visit Turin, as the temperatures start to cool down, and the city is less crowded than in summer. The foliage in the surrounding hills and parks turns vibrant shades of orange and red, creating picturesque landscapes.

Key Events:

Tuttosposi: Held in October at the Lingotto Fiere (Via Nizza, 280, 10126 Torino), this wedding fair showcases the latest trends in bridal fashion, accessories, and planning services. It's a great event if you're planning a wedding or just enjoy fashion exhibitions.

Festa della Zucca (Pumpkin Festival): Celebrated in November in the city's parks and piazzas, this festival features pumpkin-themed dishes, crafts, and family-friendly activities. Piazza Gran Madre di Dio is often the central hub for this vibrant festival.

Winter (December to February)

Winter in Turin is cold, with temperatures ranging from -1°C to 8°C (30°F to 46°F). Snowfall is not uncommon, which adds a picturesque quality to the city. While it might be chilly, winter is a magical time to experience Turin's holiday season.

Key Events:

Mercatino di Natale: From late November to December, the Christmas market in Piazza Castello transforms the square into a festive wonderland with artisan stalls, seasonal treats, and holiday decorations. It's the perfect place to find unique gifts and enjoy mulled wine and traditional sweets.

Torino Film Festival: Taking place in November, this event features screenings of independent films from around the globe. It's held at various venues, including the Cinema Massimo (Via Giuseppe Verdi, 18, 10124 Torino), and attracts cinema aficionados and filmmakers alike.

Chapter 2: Exploring Turin's Historic Heart

Piazza Castello & The Royal Palace: The Heart of Turin's Grandeur

The Splendor of Piazza Castello

Piazza Castello is the quintessential grand square, framed by majestic buildings that tell stories of a bygone era. The square's expansive layout, with its sweeping views and elegant architecture, offers a picturesque introduction to Turin's opulent history.

Address: Piazza Castello, 10123 Turin, Italy

As you step onto the piazza, you'll be greeted by the imposing façade of the Royal Palace of Turin (Palazzo Reale), an architectural masterpiece that has been the centerpiece of the city's regal splendor. Constructed in the 16th century for the House of Savoy, the palace was the residence of the Savoy dynasty and remains a symbol of the city's royal heritage.

The Royal Palace of Turin

The Royal Palace of Turin is a sprawling complex of baroque architecture, adorned with intricate stucco work, lavish interiors, and meticulously landscaped gardens. The palace served as the residence of the Dukes and later Kings of Savoy, and its opulent design reflects their wealth and taste.

Address: Piazza Castello, 10122 Turin, Italy

Upon entering the Royal Palace, visitors are immediately struck by the grandeur of the Hall of Mirrors (Sala delle Udienze), where the opulence of the Savoy court is on full display. The palace's lavish rooms, including the Throne Room and the Chapel of the Holy Shroud, are adorned with exquisite frescoes, ornate chandeliers, and magnificent tapestries.

The palace also houses the Royal Armoury, which boasts an impressive collection of arms and armor used by the Savoy dynasty. This collection offers a fascinating glimpse into the martial history of the region.

The Palace Gardens and The Armeria Reale

The palace gardens, known as the Royal Gardens (Giardini Reali), provide a serene escape from the bustling city. Designed in the 17th century, these gardens feature neatly manicured lawns, elegant fountains, and statues that enhance the palace's regal atmosphere.

The Armeria Reale, located within the palace grounds, is another must-visit. This museum showcases an extensive collection of historical weaponry and armor, offering insights into the military history of the Savoy family.

Address: Armeria Reale, Piazza Castello, 10122 Turin, Italy

Nearby Attractions

Adjacent to Piazza Castello is the Palazzo Madama, an imposing structure that combines medieval and baroque elements. Originally a Roman gate, it was transformed into a noble residence and later became the seat of the Senate of the Kingdom of Italy. Today, it houses the Museum of Ancient Art, featuring a rich collection of sculptures, paintings, and artifacts from the medieval and Renaissance periods.

Address: Piazza Castello, 10122 Turin, Italy

Practical Information

Opening Hours: The Royal Palace is typically open from Tuesday to Sunday, from 9:00 AM to 7:00 PM. It is closed on Mondays. The Armeria Reale follows similar hours.

Admission Fees: Entrance to the Royal Palace and the Armeria Reale usually requires a combined ticket. Check current prices and any special discounts or free entry days before your visit.

Getting There: Piazza Castello is centrally located and easily accessible by public transportation. You can take tram lines 4 and 7 or buses 9, 15, and 56 to reach the piazza. The area is also well-served by Turin's metro system.

Mole Antonelliana & National Cinema Museum: Icons of Italian Cinema and Culture

Location and Exterior:

Situated at Via Montebello, 20, the Mole Antonelliana rises majestically above Turin's skyline. Its unique silhouette, marked by a towering spire that reaches a height of 167 meters (547 feet), is one of the tallest masonry structures in the world. The exterior of the Mole, clad in pinkish bricks and crowned with an elegant copper spire, offers a visual treat, especially when illuminated at night.

Interior and Museum Experience:

Entering the Mole Antonelliana is like stepping into a different era. The interior of the building, with its grand hall and sweeping staircases, is as awe-inspiring as the exterior. The National Cinema Museum, which occupies the Mole's spacious interiors, is a celebration of Italy's rich cinematic heritage and is one of the most comprehensive film museums globally.

Exhibits and Collections:

The museum's exhibits are both extensive and eclectic, spanning the history of cinema from its inception to contemporary times. The museum is divided into several sections, each dedicated to different aspects of film history and technology.

Cinema and the City: This section explores the relationship between cinema and urban development, showcasing how cities have been represented in films and how films have influenced perceptions of cities.

The History of Cinema: A deep dive into the evolution of film technology and storytelling, featuring everything from early silent films to the latest digital innovations.

The Magic Lantern: An exploration of pre-cinematic visual devices, including early projectors and animated devices that paved the way for modern cinema.

The Italian Cinema: Dedicated to Italian film, this section highlights the works of iconic directors like Federico Fellini, Michelangelo Antonioni, and Roberto Rossellini, offering a comprehensive look at Italy's contribution to global cinema.

Film Techniques and Special Effects: An interactive space where visitors can learn about special effects and practical techniques used in filmmaking.

Unique Features:

One of the most captivating features of the museum is the panoramic elevator, which takes visitors up through the Mole's spire to a breathtaking observation deck. From here, you can enjoy a 360-degree view of Turin and the surrounding Alpine landscape—a spectacular sight that adds a touch of adventure to your museum visit.

Practical Information:

Opening Hours: The museum is generally open daily from 9:00 AM to 8:00 PM, with extended hours on weekends. It's advisable to check the official website for any seasonal variations or special events.

Admission: Tickets are priced at approximately €12 for adults, with reduced rates for seniors, students, and children. A combination ticket that includes access to both the Mole Antonelliana and the museum is available.

Accessibility: The museum is accessible to visitors with disabilities, with elevators and ramps available throughout the building.

Getting There: The Mole Antonelliana is centrally located and easily reachable by public transport. You can take the metro to the "Porta Nuova" station and then walk for about 15 minutes, or use the tram services that stop nearby.

Via Roma & Piazza San Carlo: Strolling through Turin's Elegant Shopping Streets

Via Roma: A Shopper's Paradise

As you stroll down Via Roma, you're greeted by a long row of portico-lined streets that provide both a visual and physical shelter from the hustle and bustle of the city. The porticos, designed by architect Alessandro Antonelli in the 19th century, not only protect you from the elements but also add a timeless grace to this iconic street.

This avenue is a shopping haven, boasting a mix of high-end boutiques and flagship stores. Start your exploration at the Galleria San Federico (Via Roma 8), a beautifully restored shopping gallery that houses some of the most prestigious Italian and international brands. Inside, you'll find elegant shops like Gucci (Via Roma 28), where luxury meets sophistication, and Louis Vuitton (Via Roma 36), known for its classic yet contemporary designs.

Further along Via Roma, the grandeur of La Rinascente (Via Roma 10) awaits. This renowned department store offers a comprehensive selection of fashion, beauty products, and gourmet food. Take the escalator up to the rooftop café, where you can enjoy a panoramic view of the city while sipping on a perfectly brewed espresso.

For a more unique shopping experience, visit Caffè Torino (Piazza San Carlo 204), an elegant café where you can take a break from shopping. Here, you'll find traditional pastries and a variety of coffee blends, perfect for recharging before continuing your retail adventure.

Piazza San Carlo: The Living Room of Turin

At the end of Via Roma lies Piazza San Carlo, often referred to as the "Living Room" of Turin. This grand square, framed by twin baroque churches—Santa Cristina and San Carlo

Borromeo—is a masterpiece of urban design. The open space, flanked by historic arcades and elegant buildings, exudes a sense of opulence and tranquility.

The square is home to several important landmarks, including the Equestrian Statue of Emmanuel Philibert (in the center of the square). This statue honors the Duke of Savoy, who played a crucial role in Turin's history. Surrounding the statue are historic cafés like Caffè San Carlo (Piazza San Carlo 156), which has been serving patrons since 1822. Its classic interior and refined atmosphere make it a perfect spot for people-watching or enjoying a leisurely coffee.

Adjacent to Piazza San Carlo, you'll find Piazza Carlo Alberto (Piazza Carlo Alberto), which houses the Museo Egizio (Via Accademia delle Scienze 6). While not a shopping destination, this museum is one of Turin's crown jewels and provides an excellent complement to your day exploring the city's commercial heart.

Practical Tips

Best Time to Visit: Weekdays are ideal for a relaxed shopping experience, while weekends can be more crowded. Early morning or late afternoon visits allow you to enjoy the city at a more leisurely pace.

Getting There: Via Roma is easily accessible via Turin's public transport system. The Porta Nuova train station is a short walk away, and several bus and tram lines service the area.

Dress Code: Turin is known for its stylish residents, so dressing smartly will help you blend in and enhance your shopping experience.

Chapter 3: Art and Culture in Turin

Museo Egizio: The World's Finest Egyptian Collection Outside Egypt

Historical Significance

Founded in 1824 by the House of Savoy, the Museo Egizio began with a collection of artifacts acquired during the Napoleonic era. Over the years, it has expanded dramatically, largely thanks to the efforts of Italian archaeologists and collectors. The museum's rich collection reflects Turin's historical ties with Egypt, particularly through the work of Giovanni Battista Belzoni, an Italian explorer who made significant contributions to the collection.

The Collection

The museum houses over 30,000 artifacts, ranging from monumental statues to intricate jewelry. The collection is organized into several thematic sections, each offering a unique perspective on ancient Egyptian life and culture.

1. The Sarcophagi and Mummies

One of the highlights of the Museo Egizio is its impressive collection of sarcophagi and mummies. The display provides insight into the ancient Egyptian burial practices and the art of mummification. The most notable is the mummy of Kha and Merit, a high-ranking couple whose well-preserved remains offer a rare look into the life of the elite during the New Kingdom period (circa 1550–1070 BCE). The sarcophagus of Kha, a royal architect, is adorned with detailed hieroglyphics and exquisite craftsmanship that reflects his prestigious status.

Location in the Museum: The sarcophagi and mummies are prominently displayed in the main hall, where they are arranged chronologically, allowing visitors to trace the evolution of burial practices.

2. The Papyrus Collection

The museum's papyrus collection is among the most extensive in the world. It includes religious texts, magical spells, and administrative documents that provide a window into the everyday life and spiritual practices of ancient Egyptians. Notable among these is the Book of the Dead, a collection of spells intended to guide the deceased through the afterlife. The museum's papyrus is displayed in a climate-controlled environment to preserve its fragile state, with detailed translations and explanations available for those interested in delving deeper into the texts.

Location in the Museum: The papyrus collection is housed in a dedicated gallery on the upper floor, where visitors can view the scrolls and their translations.

3. Statues and Sculptures

The museum's collection of statues and sculptures showcases the grandeur of ancient Egyptian art. Highlights include the imposing statue of Ramses II, known for his military prowess and architectural achievements. Another notable piece is the statue of Sekhmet, the lion-headed goddess of war and healing. These sculptures not only demonstrate the artistic skills of ancient Egyptian craftsmen but also provide insight into the religious and political life of the time.

Location in the Museum: The statues and sculptures are displayed in a large central hall, arranged thematically by deity, pharaoh, and purpose.

4. Everyday Life and Crafts

In addition to monumental artifacts, the museum features a collection of everyday objects that illustrate daily life in ancient Egypt. This includes jewelry, tools, and pottery, as well as items related to daily activities such as cooking and writing. The section on ancient Egyptian crafts highlights the techniques used to create items from materials like faience and alabaster.

Location in the Museum: This collection is located in a series of smaller, thematic rooms adjacent to the main exhibit halls, providing a more intimate look at the material culture of ancient Egypt.

Visitor Experience

Exhibits and Tours

The Museo Egizio offers a range of exhibits and educational tours designed to enhance the visitor experience. Audio guides are available in multiple languages, providing detailed commentary on the exhibits. For those interested in a deeper dive, guided tours led by knowledgeable experts offer comprehensive insights into specific aspects of the collection. The museum also hosts temporary exhibitions that explore various themes related to ancient Egyptian culture.

Tour Information: Tours can be booked in advance through the museum's official website or at the ticket counter. Check for special thematic tours or events during your visit.

Museum Facilities

The museum provides several amenities to enhance your visit. There is a well-stocked gift shop offering a range of souvenirs, including replicas of artifacts and books on Egyptian history. The museum café serves light refreshments and provides a pleasant spot to relax and reflect on your visit.

Café Location: The café is located on the ground floor, near the entrance, making it a convenient stop before or after exploring the exhibits.

Practical Information

Opening Hours and Admission

The Museo Egizio is open daily from 9:00 AM to 6:30 PM, with extended hours on Thursdays until 10:00 PM. It is closed on Mondays. Admission fees are reasonable, with discounts available for students, seniors, and groups. The museum also offers free admission on the first Sunday of each month.

Ticket Information: Tickets can be purchased at the museum's entrance or in advance through their website. Booking online is recommended to avoid long queues.

Getting There

The Museo Egizio is centrally located in Turin and is easily accessible by public transportation. The nearest metro station is Porta Nuova, which is a short walk from the museum. Buses and trams also serve the area, with several stops nearby.

Public Transportation: The museum is well-served by Turin's public transport system, making it easy to reach from various parts of the city.

Galleria Sabauda: Masterpieces of the Savoy Dynasty

A Historical Overview

The origins of the Galleria Sabauda can be traced back to the 19th century when King Carlo Alberto of Savoy began collecting art to enhance the royal collections. This initial collection was further enriched by his successors, who added works from various periods, including the Renaissance and Baroque eras. In 1832, the gallery was officially opened to the public, showcasing an impressive array of artworks that reflected the artistic and cultural significance of the Savoy Dynasty.

The Gallery's Layout and Architecture

Entering the Galleria Sabauda, visitors are greeted by an opulent setting that complements the artistic treasures within. The gallery is housed in the Royal Palace, a magnificent Baroque edifice with a facade that reflects the grandeur of the Savoy reign. The museum's interior features high ceilings adorned with frescoes, intricate moldings, and expansive galleries that provide the perfect backdrop for the collection.

The gallery is divided into several rooms, each dedicated to different periods and styles. The layout is designed to take visitors on a chronological journey through art history, from the early Renaissance to the 18th century. The spacious rooms allow for an immersive experience, giving each artwork the space to be appreciated fully.

Masterpieces and Notable Works

1. "The Annunciation" by Sandro Botticelli

One of the gallery's crown jewels is Sandro Botticelli's The Annunciation. Painted in the late 15th century, this work exemplifies Botticelli's delicate style and mastery of form. The painting captures the angel Gabriel announcing to the Virgin Mary that she will conceive the Son of God. The ethereal quality of the figures and the detailed backgrounds reflect Botticelli's skill in combining naturalism with divine themes.

Location: Room 7

Address: Galleria Sabauda, Piazza Castello, 10122 Turin, Italy

2. "Portrait of a Lady with a Unicorn" by Raphael

Another highlight is Raphael's Portrait of a Lady with a Unicorn. This exquisite portrait demonstrates Raphael's finesse in capturing the subtleties of human expression and the richness of textures. The unicorn, a symbol of purity, adds a layer of symbolic meaning to the piece. The painting's elegance and detail showcase why Raphael is considered one of the Renaissance's great masters.

Location: Room 9

Address: Galleria Sabauda, Piazza Castello, 10122 Turin, Italy

3. "The Holy Family with Saint John the Baptist" by Michelangelo

Michelangelo's The Holy Family with Saint John the Baptist is a masterpiece of Renaissance art. Known for its intricate composition and powerful figures, this work displays

Michelangelo's characteristic attention to anatomical precision and dramatic intensity. The depiction of the Holy Family and the young John the Baptist is rendered with a grace that highlights Michelangelo's artistic genius.

Location: Room 10

Address: Galleria Sabauda, Piazza Castello, 10122 Turin, Italy

4. "The Last Supper" by Giampietrino

While not as famous as Leonardo da Vinci's The Last Supper, Giampietrino's copy of the masterpiece offers a unique perspective. Created in the 16th century, this work provides invaluable insight into the original fresco, which was significantly damaged over time. The detailed reproduction helps visitors understand the grandeur of the original piece and its historical context.

Location: Room 12

Address: Galleria Sabauda, Piazza Castello, 10122 Turin, Italy

Special Exhibitions and Events

The Galleria Sabauda frequently hosts special exhibitions and events that offer deeper insights into its collection and art history. These exhibitions often feature works from other renowned museums or focus on specific themes or artists. The gallery's website and local event listings provide up-to-date information on current and upcoming exhibitions.

Special Exhibitions Schedule: Check the gallery's official website or visit the information desk upon arrival for the latest updates.

Website: Galleria Sabauda Official Website

Visitor Information

Opening Hours: The gallery is generally open Tuesday to Sunday from 9:00 AM to 7:00 PM, with extended hours during special exhibitions. It is closed on Mondays.

Admission: Tickets can be purchased at the entrance or online. General admission is approximately €10, with reduced rates for students and seniors.

Address: Piazza Castello, 10122 Turin, Italy

Phone: +39 011 436 1455

Public Transport: The Galleria Sabauda is easily accessible by public transportation. The nearest metro station is Porta Nuova, and several bus lines stop at Piazza Castello.

Accessibility: The gallery is wheelchair accessible, with elevators and ramps available for visitors with mobility issues.

Contemporary Art Scene: Where to Find Modern Creativity

Fondazione Sandretto Re Rebaudengo

Address: Via Modane, 16, 10141 Torino TO, Italy

One of Turin's most influential contemporary art institutions, the Fondazione Sandretto Re Rebaudengo, is a must-visit for art enthusiasts. Established in 1995 by collector and philanthropist Patrizia Sandretto Re Rebaudengo, this foundation is known for its bold exhibitions and support of emerging artists. The foundation's striking architectural space, designed by Claudio Silvestrin, provides a minimalist backdrop that allows the art to take center stage.

The foundation's exhibitions often feature international artists working across various media, from painting and sculpture to video and installation art. Their rotating exhibitions offer fresh perspectives on contemporary art and reflect the latest trends and discussions in the art world. Additionally, the foundation regularly hosts workshops, lectures, and art talks, providing a deeper engagement with the art on display.

Museo d'Arte Contemporanea di Rivoli (Castello di Rivoli)

Address: Piazza Mafalda di Savoia, 1, 10098 Rivoli TO, Italy

Website: castellodirivoli.org

Located just outside of central Turin, the Museo d'Arte Contemporanea di Rivoli, housed in the historic Castello di Rivoli, is a cornerstone of contemporary art in the region. The museum's collection spans from the late 20th century to the present, showcasing works by prominent international artists. The juxtaposition of contemporary art within a historic castle setting creates a unique viewing experience.

The museum's permanent collection includes pieces by artists such as Damien Hirst, Anish Kapoor, and Cindy Sherman, while its temporary exhibitions frequently highlight emerging artists and innovative practices. The museum also offers educational programs and workshops, making it a hub for both art aficionados and those new to contemporary art.

Galleria d'Arte Moderna e Contemporanea (GAM)

Address: Via Magenta, 31, 10128 Torino TO, Italy

Website: gamtorino.it

GAM, or the Galleria d'Arte Moderna e Contemporanea, is another key player in Turin's art scene. While the gallery's collection includes works from the 19th century, its contemporary art holdings are particularly noteworthy. GAM's contemporary collection features works by Italian and international artists, reflecting the gallery's commitment to showcasing a diverse range of artistic practices.

The gallery's exhibitions are carefully curated to offer insight into current trends and movements in contemporary art. GAM also organizes special events, including artist talks and guided tours, which enhance the visitor experience and provide a deeper understanding of the art on display.

Spazio 42

Address: Via Gabriele D'Annunzio, 42, 10126 Torino TO, Italy

Website: spazio42.com

Spazio 42 is an independent contemporary art space that has gained recognition for its experimental approach and commitment to showcasing innovative art. Located in a former industrial building, the space provides a raw, unpolished environment that complements the bold, contemporary artworks it hosts.

The gallery's program is diverse, featuring solo exhibitions, group shows, and site-specific installations. Spazio 42 often collaborates with artists, curators, and institutions to produce thought-provoking exhibitions that challenge conventional artistic boundaries. It's a place where you can discover the latest trends and movements in the art world while engaging with artists directly.

Murazzi del Po

Address: Murazzi del Po, 10125 Torino TO, Italy

The Murazzi del Po, the historic riverside embankment along the Po River, has evolved into a vibrant cultural hotspot where contemporary art intersects with urban life. The area features an array of street art and murals that add a dynamic, colorful layer to the city's visual landscape.

Local and international street artists use the Murazzi as a canvas to express their creativity, often addressing social and political themes through their work. Walking along the Murazzi del Po, you'll encounter a constantly changing gallery of street art that reflects the city's diverse artistic expressions.

The Art Gallery of Modern Art (GAM) at Palazzo Chiablese

Address: Via XX Settembre, 3, 10121 Torino TO, Italy

Website: gamtorino.it

Situated in the elegant Palazzo Chiablese, this section of GAM focuses on modern and contemporary art in a historical setting. The gallery's collection includes a range of artworks from the 20th century to the present, showcasing the evolution of artistic practices over time.

The gallery's exhibitions often explore themes related to modernity and contemporary issues, offering visitors a chance to engage with art that reflects current social and cultural dynamics. The Palazzo Chiablese's historic charm provides a unique backdrop for the gallery's contemporary collections.

Fiorucci Art Trust

Address: Via Giovanni da Verrazzano, 18, 10128 Torino TO, Italy

Website: fiorucciarttrust.com

The Fiorucci Art Trust is a private collection and exhibition space dedicated to contemporary art. Founded by art collector and philanthropist Elio Fiorucci, the trust focuses on supporting and showcasing emerging and established artists from around the world. The collection is known for its eclectic mix of art, from provocative installations to experimental video works.

Exhibitions at the Fiorucci Art Trust often push boundaries and challenge traditional art forms, providing a platform for innovative and thought-provoking art. Visitors to the trust can experience a diverse range of artistic practices and engage with some of the most exciting voices in contemporary art.

Chapter 4: Savoring Turin's Culinary Delights

Piazza Vittorio Veneto's Cafés: Sip Espresso Like a Local

1. Caffè al Bicerin

Address: Piazza della Consolata 5, 10122 Torino, Italy

Established in 1763, Caffè al Bicerin is not just a café; it's a living piece of Turin's history. Located slightly off the square, this intimate café is renowned for its eponymous drink, the Bicerin. This traditional Turinese beverage is a luscious blend of espresso, chocolate, and whipped cream, served in a glass so you can appreciate its layered beauty. The Bicerin has been enjoyed by locals and visitors alike for over two centuries, including notable figures like Alexandre Dumas and Friedrich Nietzsche.

The café's décor harks back to the 18th century, with wooden tables, vintage mirrors, and brass fittings that evoke a timeless elegance. As you savor your Bicerin, take a moment to soak in the café's rich history and the warmth of its atmosphere. The staff here are exceptionally knowledgeable and eager to share the story behind their signature drink.

2. Caffè Fiorio

Address: Via Po 8, 10124 Torino, Italy

Caffè Fiorio, established in 1780, is another cornerstone of Turin's café culture. Located just a short walk from Piazza Vittorio Veneto, it's a quintessential destination for those seeking a classic Italian coffee experience. The café is famous for its elegant interior, complete with antique chandeliers and a charming, old-world ambiance.

Caffè Fiorio is known for its outstanding espresso, made from a blend of carefully selected beans roasted to perfection. It also offers a range of pastries and desserts, including its celebrated torta di nocciole, a delightful hazelnut cake that pairs perfectly with a cup of strong coffee. The café's outdoor seating provides a splendid view of the historic Via Po, making it a fantastic spot to watch the world go by while enjoying your espresso.

3. Caffè Torino

Address: Piazza San Carlo 204, 10121 Torino, Italy

Caffè Torino is another gem located near Piazza Vittorio Veneto, situated on the bustling Piazza San Carlo. Founded in 1903, this café is renowned for its luxurious setting and rich coffee heritage. The décor is a blend of Art Nouveau elegance with modern touches, featuring plush seating and intricate details that create an inviting atmosphere.

At Caffè Torino, you can experience the city's coffee culture in style. The espresso here is expertly brewed, with a strong, aromatic flavor that is a hallmark of Turin's coffee tradition. In addition to excellent coffee, the café offers a selection of sophisticated pastries and light meals, perfect for a leisurely breakfast or a mid-afternoon treat. The outdoor terrace is ideal for enjoying your coffee while taking in the lively ambiance of Piazza San Carlo.

4. Caffè Roma

Address: Via Roma 276, 10121 Torino, Italy

Caffè Roma, situated along Via Roma, is a popular spot among locals for its vibrant atmosphere and quality coffee. Established in the 1930s, this café has maintained its reputation for serving excellent espresso and providing a welcoming space for socializing. The interior is modern yet comfortable, with a design that reflects both contemporary and traditional elements.

The café's espresso is a true delight, offering a rich and robust flavor that captures the essence of Italian coffee. Caffè Roma is also known for its delicious cornetti, Italian croissants that are fresh and buttery, making it a great place for a relaxed breakfast or a quick coffee break. The café's central location makes it a convenient choice for a coffee stop while exploring the city.

5. Caffè Verdi

Address: Via Garibaldi 25, 10122 Torino, Italy

Caffè Verdi, located on the lively Via Garibaldi, is a must-visit for those looking to experience a blend of modern vibrancy and traditional charm. Established in the mid-20th century, this café offers a contemporary take on Turin's coffee culture. The interior is sleek and stylish, with clean lines and a bright, airy feel.

The espresso at Caffè Verdi is known for its smooth, balanced flavor, achieved through a meticulous brewing process. The café also offers a variety of specialty coffees and an array of sweet and savory snacks. The large windows provide a great vantage point to observe the bustling street life outside, making it an excellent spot for people-watching while enjoying your coffee.

Experiencing Piazza Vittorio Veneto

Piazza Vittorio Veneto is more than just a place to enjoy coffee; it's an experience that captures the essence of Turin. The square itself is a lively hub, often hosting local events, markets, and cultural activities. Its expansive layout and historic charm make it an ideal location to immerse yourself in the city's atmosphere.

As you visit these cafés, you'll discover that Turin's coffee culture is not just about the drink itself but also about the experience of savoring it in a setting that reflects the city's rich heritage. Whether you're indulging in a Bicerin at Caffè al Bicerin, enjoying a classic espresso at Caffè Fiorio, or taking in the lively ambiance at Caffè Roma, each café offers a unique way to connect with the heart of Turin.

Eataly Turin: A Gastronomic Journey in One Place

Location and Ambiance

Address: Eataly Turin, Piazza Solferino 1, 10121 Turin, Italy

Eataly Turin occupies a historic building in Piazza Solferino, a central location that is easily accessible from all corners of the city. The store's design seamlessly marries contemporary aesthetics with traditional Italian charm. Upon entering, you're greeted by a bustling atmosphere filled with the enticing aromas of freshly baked bread, rich cheeses, and sizzling meats. The spacious layout is divided into various sections, each dedicated to different aspects of Italian cuisine, making it easy to navigate and explore.

Culinary Offerings

Fresh Produce and Deli

One of the standout features of Eataly Turin is its expansive fresh produce section. Here, you'll find a vibrant array of fruits and vegetables sourced from local farmers and artisanal producers. The market's commitment to quality is evident in every corner, with organic and seasonal options prominently displayed.

The deli section offers an impressive selection of cured meats, cheeses, and prepared foods. From succulent prosciutto di Parma to tangy gorgonzola, the variety is vast and the quality is impeccable. For a true taste of Italy, don't miss the chance to sample some freshly made mortadella or a wheel of Parmigiano-Reggiano, aged to perfection.

Bakery and Pastry

The bakery at Eataly Turin is a sensory delight, with an array of freshly baked breads, pastries, and desserts. The scent of warm focaccia and croissants fills the air, tempting you to indulge in their delectable offerings. The pastries are a particular highlight, with traditional Italian treats like cannoli, sfogliatella, and tiramisu available for purchase. Each item is crafted with care, using high-quality ingredients and traditional methods.

Gourmet Grocery

The grocery section of Eataly Turin is a treasure trove of Italian culinary staples. Here, you'll find an extensive selection of pasta, sauces, olive oils, and vinegars, as well as a diverse range of international gourmet products. The store's commitment to quality is reflected in its curated selection of artisanal products, including hand-crafted pasta and small-batch sauces.

One must-try is the house-made pasta, available in various shapes and flavors. The store's knowledgeable staff can offer recommendations and pairing suggestions, ensuring you find the perfect ingredients for your culinary creations.

Restaurants and Dining

Eataly Turin is home to several dining establishments, each offering a unique culinary experience. These include:

Ristorante Smeraldo: A refined restaurant that focuses on traditional Italian dishes with a modern twist. Here, you can enjoy expertly crafted dishes such as risotto with truffle, or a perfectly grilled steak, all made with ingredients sourced directly from the market.

La Piazza: A casual eatery that features a rotating menu of seasonal dishes. This is a great spot for a quick and satisfying meal, whether you're in the mood for a hearty pasta dish or a refreshing salad.

Osteria del Vino: An excellent choice for wine lovers, this restaurant offers an extensive wine list featuring selections from all over Italy. Pair your meal with a carefully chosen wine from the store's cellar for a truly memorable dining experience.

Special Events and Workshops

Eataly Turin is not just a place to shop and eat; it's also a hub of culinary education and cultural events. The store regularly hosts cooking classes, wine tastings, and food-themed workshops, offering visitors a chance to learn from expert chefs and artisans. These events cover a wide range of topics, from mastering the art of pasta-making to exploring regional Italian cuisines.

To stay updated on upcoming events, check Eataly's website or visit their information desk upon arrival. Participation in these workshops provides an opportunity to delve deeper into Italy's culinary traditions and gain hands-on experience in the kitchen.

Tips for Visiting

Timing: Eataly Turin can get quite busy, especially on weekends and during lunchtime. To avoid crowds, consider visiting during weekdays or early in the morning.

Sampling: Don't hesitate to ask for samples, especially at the deli and bakery sections. The staff are knowledgeable and happy to provide tastes of their products, allowing you to make informed choices.

Shopping: If you're planning to purchase groceries or gifts, remember that Eataly offers a wide selection of packaged items that are perfect for taking home. Be sure to explore the shelves for unique Italian products.

Dining: Reservations are recommended for the sit-down restaurants, particularly during peak hours. This will ensure you get a table and can enjoy a leisurely meal without any hassle.

Chocolate Heaven: Gianduiotto and the Birthplace of Nutella

The Origins of Gianduiotto

Gianduiotto, Turin's signature chocolate, has a history that dates back to the early 19th century. Named after Gianduja, a character from the Commedia dell'Arte, Gianduiotto is a smooth, creamy chocolate confection enriched with a generous amount of finely ground hazelnuts. This blend of chocolate and nuts is said to have been created during the Napoleonic era when cocoa was scarce due to trade blockades. Italian chocolatiers, resourceful as ever, began incorporating locally grown hazelnuts to create a richer, more flavorful chocolate.

One of the earliest and most renowned producers of gianduiotto is Caffarel, established in 1826 by the enterprising Pietro Caffarel. Located at Via Luigi Cibrario, 14, 10144 Torino, this historic chocolatier remains a landmark of Turin's confectionery heritage. Stepping into the Caffarel store is like taking a journey back in time, with its elegantly preserved interiors and an array of artisanal chocolates that showcase the traditional methods passed down through generations.

Another must-visit for gianduiotto enthusiasts is Venchi, founded in 1878. The Venchi store at Via Roma, 6, 10121 Torino offers a modern twist on the classic gianduiotto. Their chocolates are crafted using high-quality cocoa beans and Piedmont hazelnuts, ensuring that each bite is as exquisite as the last. Venchi's store, with its sleek, contemporary design and extensive range of chocolate products, is a testament to Turin's enduring love affair with chocolate.

Nutella: From Turin to the World

While gianduiotto has been a cherished local treat, Nutella has taken the world by storm. The creation of Nutella is attributed to the Ferrero family, who started their chocolate-making journey in the small town of Alba, not far from Turin. In 1964, Ferrero introduced Nutella, a creamy blend of cocoa, sugar, and hazelnuts that has since become a household name.

The Ferrero headquarters, Piazza Vittorio Veneto, 12, 12051 Alba (CN), is not open to the public, but the Ferrero Museum, located in the nearby town of Alba, offers a fascinating insight into the history and production of Nutella. The museum, officially known as the Ferrero Chocolate Museum, showcases the evolution of the company and its iconic products. Visitors can explore interactive exhibits, watch videos on the chocolate-making process, and even sample some of Ferrero's delicious creations.

Where to Experience Chocolate in Turin

If you're visiting Turin, a chocolate pilgrimage is a must. Here are some top spots where you can indulge in Turin's chocolate legacy:

Caffarel: Located at Via Luigi Cibrario, 14, Caffarel's flagship store is a treasure trove of traditional chocolates. Don't miss their gianduiotto, which is made using a classic recipe. The store also offers a range of other chocolate treats and specialties that are perfect for gifts or personal indulgence.

Venchi: Situated at Via Roma, 6, Venchi's store is a chocolate lover's paradise. Here, you can sample their innovative gianduiotto variations and explore a range of artisanal chocolates. The store's sleek design and modern approach to chocolate-making make it a unique destination in Turin.

La Casa del Gianduiotto: Located at Via Garibaldi, 25, this charming shop specializes in gianduiotto and other Piedmontese confections. The shop's cozy atmosphere and friendly staff make it a perfect place to learn more about the history of gianduiotto while enjoying some freshly made chocolates.

Baratti & Milano: Situated at Piazza Castello, 6, Baratti & Milano has been a staple of Turin's chocolate scene since 1858. Their elegant café offers a variety of chocolate treats, including their signature gianduiotto. Enjoy a cup of hot chocolate or a sweet pastry while soaking in the historic ambiance of this classic establishment.

Cioccolato Peyrano: Found at Corso Moncalieri, 34, Peyrano is another historic name in Turin's chocolate history. The shop offers a range of high-quality chocolates, including gianduiotto, and is known for its artisanal approach to confectionery.

Chocolate Tours and Experiences

For those looking to delve deeper into Turin's chocolate culture, consider joining a guided chocolate tour. These tours offer a behind-the-scenes look at local chocolate makers and provide tastings of some of the best chocolates Turin has to offer. Turin Chocolate Tours, based in the city center, offers comprehensive tours that include visits to multiple chocolate shops, historical insights, and plenty of opportunities to sample and savor.

Additionally, check out local food festivals such as the CioccolaTò held annually in Turin. This chocolate festival showcases the best of Italian and international chocolate and is a great way to experience the city's passion for sweets.

Chapter 5: Hidden Gems and Local Favorites

The Balon Market: Vintage Finds and Antiques Galore

A Brief History

The Balon Market boasts a storied history dating back to the 19th century when it began as a modest flea market. Over time, it evolved into one of the largest and most renowned antique markets in Italy. Its name, "Balon," derives from the local dialect term for "ball," referencing the traditional ball games played in the area. Today, the market is a lively testament to Turin's rich cultural heritage and the enduring appeal of vintage finds.

Exploring the Market

The Balon Market stretches along the Via Borgo Dora and its surrounding streets, and its sheer size can be both exciting and overwhelming. The market is open from 9:00 AM to 5:00 PM every Saturday, with a smaller, more intimate version taking place on the first Sunday of the month. Arriving early is advisable, as the best finds often go quickly.

Vintage Clothing and Accessories: One of the highlights of the Balon Market is its impressive array of vintage clothing and accessories. Stalls overflow with stylish garments from past decades, including elegant 1950s dresses, tailored 1960s suits, and chic 1980s jackets. Look for stands run by local vintage enthusiasts such as Vintage Vintner, located near the corner of Via Borgo Dora and Piazza della Repubblica. They offer a curated selection of timeless pieces that reflect the fashion trends of yesteryears.

Antique Furniture and Home Décor: If you're on the hunt for antique furniture or unique home décor items, the Balon Market is a goldmine. You'll find everything from ornate Baroque-style armchairs to rustic country tables. For exquisite pieces with a storied past, check out Antiquariato J&L, located at Via Borgo Dora 35. This stall is renowned for its high-quality furniture and eclectic assortment of vintage lamps, mirrors, and artwork.

Collectibles and Memorabilia: The market is also a fantastic place to find rare collectibles and memorabilia. Whether you're interested in old vinyl records, vintage cameras, or retro toys, there's something for every collector. Head to Collezionismo Torino, situated at Via Borgo Dora 45, to browse their impressive collection of coins, stamps, and historical artifacts.

Jewelry and Accessories: For those with an eye for unique jewelry, the Balon Market offers an array of antique and vintage pieces. From Art Deco brooches to classic cameo pendants, the selection is diverse. Gioielli Antichi di Laura, found near Piazza della Repubblica, is a must-visit for anyone looking to add a touch of historical elegance to their collection.

Navigating the Market

While the Balon Market is a delightful experience, it can also be a bit chaotic, especially during peak hours. Here are some tips to help you navigate and enjoy your visit:

Wear Comfortable Shoes: The market is spread out, and you'll likely be on your feet for several hours. Comfortable shoes are essential for exploring all the stalls and shops.

Bring Cash: Many vendors do not accept credit cards, so it's a good idea to carry cash. ATMs are available in the vicinity, but having some cash on hand will make transactions smoother.

Bargain Politely: Haggling is a common practice at the Balon Market. Don't hesitate to negotiate prices, but always do so respectfully. Many vendors are open to reasonable offers, especially if you're buying multiple items.

Take Your Time: The market's charm lies in its variety and the thrill of discovery. Allow yourself plenty of time to explore each stall and uncover hidden gems. Patience often leads to the best finds.

Beyond the Market: What to See and Do

While the Balon Market is a major draw, the Quadrilatero Romano district itself is worth exploring. This historic area is filled with charming streets, trendy cafés, and vibrant bars. After a morning of market browsing, take some time to enjoy a leisurely lunch or coffee at one of the nearby spots.

Caffè Fiorio: Located at Via Po 20, this historic café offers a perfect spot to relax and soak in the local atmosphere. Established in 1780, Caffè Fiorio is known for its elegant ambiance and delicious pastries.

Museo del Risorgimento: Situated at Via Accademia delle Scienze 5, this museum provides an insightful look into Italy's unification history. It's a short walk from the market and offers a fascinating counterpoint to your market experience.

Via Garibaldi: One of Turin's main shopping streets, Via Garibaldi is lined with boutiques and shops, offering a blend of modern retail and historic charm. It's a great place to wander and discover more of the city's local flavor.

Borgo Medievale: A Step Back in Time Along the Po River

A Brief History

Borgo Medievale was constructed for the 1884 International Exposition of Turin, aimed at showcasing Italy's rich cultural heritage. Designed by architect Alessandro Antonelli, who is also renowned for his work on the Mole Antonelliana, the village was intended as a celebration of medieval architecture and urban planning. Although initially planned as a temporary exhibit, its popularity led to its preservation and transformation into one of Turin's most beloved historical sites.

The Village's Layout and Attractions

Via del Borgo, 30, 10131 Torino TO, Italy

Entering Borgo Medievale feels like stepping through a time portal. The village is set against the backdrop of the lush Valentino Park, providing a picturesque setting that enhances its medieval ambiance. The layout of Borgo Medievale is thoughtfully designed, with cobblestone streets, medieval houses, and a fortifying castle that offers a sense of authenticity and historical richness.

The Castle

At the heart of the Borgo is the imposing Castello Medievale. This structure, though not a genuine medieval castle, is modeled after the fortifications found in various Italian regions. Visitors can explore the castle's ramparts and towers, which offer panoramic views of the Po River and the surrounding park. Inside, the castle houses a small museum dedicated to medieval weaponry and artifacts, providing insights into the martial history of the era.

The Artisan Shops

Walking through Borgo Medievale, you'll encounter several artisan shops that sell handcrafted goods reminiscent of medieval trades. From blacksmiths and weavers to potters and coopers, these craftsmen demonstrate traditional skills and offer unique souvenirs that capture the essence of medieval craftsmanship. A highlight is the pottery workshop, where visitors can watch artisans create intricate designs using traditional techniques.

The Medieval Houses

The medieval houses in Borgo Medievale are carefully reconstructed to reflect different styles and periods. These buildings offer a glimpse into the daily lives of medieval citizens. Each house is furnished with period-appropriate artifacts and exhibits, including period furniture, cooking utensils, and textiles. Visitors can explore these homes to understand how people lived, worked, and celebrated in the Middle Ages.

The Gardens

Adjacent to the castle and medieval houses are beautifully landscaped gardens that echo the medieval period's aesthetic. The gardens are designed to replicate the types of gardens found in medieval Italian villages, featuring a variety of herbs, flowers, and medicinal plants used in the Middle Ages. Strolling through these gardens provides a serene escape and a chance to reflect on the medieval lifestyle.

Visiting Borgo Medievale

Opening Hours: Borgo Medievale is open daily from 9:00 AM to 7:00 PM, with extended hours during the summer months. The castle and museums within the village are open from 10:00 AM to 6:00 PM.

Admission Fees: The entrance fee to Borgo Medievale is approximately €6 for adults, with reduced rates for children and seniors. Admission includes access to the castle, museums, and artisan workshops. Tickets can be purchased on-site or online through the official website.

Getting There:

Borgo Medievale is easily accessible from the center of Turin. It is located within Valentino Park, a short walk from the city's main attractions. You can reach the park by taking Tram Line 9 or Bus Line 18, both of which have stops near the park entrance. Alternatively, it's a pleasant 20-minute walk from Piazza Vittorio Veneto, where you can enjoy views of the Po River along the way.

Nearby Attractions:

Valentino Park: Before or after your visit to Borgo Medievale, take time to explore Valentino Park, which offers beautiful green spaces, walking trails, and the Valentino Castle. The park is a great spot for a leisurely stroll or a picnic.

Mole Antonelliana: Just a short tram ride away, this iconic landmark offers panoramic views of the city and houses the National Museum of Cinema.

Piazza Vittorio Veneto: A lively square with numerous cafés and restaurants, perfect for a meal or coffee break.

Practical Tips

Wear Comfortable Shoes: Borgo Medievale's cobblestone streets and uneven paths make comfortable footwear essential. Sturdy walking shoes will enhance your experience.

Weather Considerations: Turin can be quite warm in the summer and chilly in the winter. Check the weather forecast and dress accordingly. Rain can make the cobblestones slippery, so bring an umbrella if needed.

Photography: Photography is allowed in most areas of Borgo Medievale. However, be mindful of any restrictions in specific exhibits or workshops.

Quadrilatero Romano: Where History and Nightlife Collide

A Walk Through History

Quadrilatero Romano's historical significance is evident as soon as you set foot in the neighborhood. The area's name reflects its origins as part of the Roman city plan, and remnants of this ancient past can still be seen throughout the district. The grid layout of the streets is a direct nod to Roman urban planning, and walking through these streets feels like stepping back in time.

Via delle Orfane is a particularly noteworthy street for history enthusiasts. This charming street is lined with beautifully preserved Baroque buildings, and at number 7, you'll find the Palazzo delle Orfane. Originally a home for orphans and abandoned children in the 17th century, this building now houses the Turin School of Fine Arts. Its grand façade and ornate interiors offer a glimpse into the architectural splendor of Turin's past.

Nearby, Piazza IV Marzo is a small square that houses the remains of the Roman Walls of Turin. These ancient fortifications once protected the city, and sections of the walls can still be seen integrated into the modern buildings. It's a fantastic spot to appreciate the contrast between the old and new, as you ponder the history that shaped this bustling area.

The Culinary Scene

No visit to Quadrilatero Romano is complete without indulging in its exceptional food scene. The neighborhood is renowned for its diverse array of restaurants and eateries, offering everything from traditional Piedmontese cuisine to contemporary dining experiences.

Ristorante del Cambio at Piazza Carignano 2 is a must-visit for those seeking a taste of luxury. Established in 1757, this historic restaurant has served as a gathering place for royalty and celebrities. The opulent interior and classic menu, featuring dishes like agnolotti del plin (Piedmontese stuffed pasta) and brasato al Barolo (Barolo wine-braised beef), provide an authentic taste of Turin's culinary heritage.

For a more casual dining experience, Eataly Torino at Piazza Solferino 1 is a gastronomic paradise. This sprawling food market and restaurant complex offers a wide range of Italian delicacies, from fresh pasta and artisanal cheeses to delectable pastries. It's an excellent place to sample local specialties and enjoy a leisurely meal.

If you're in the mood for something sweet, Cioccolateria Peyrano at Via della Consolata 1 is a chocolate lover's dream. Established in 1929, this iconic chocolatier is known for its rich, handcrafted chocolates and traditional recipes. Be sure to try their famous gianduiotto, a creamy hazelnut chocolate that originated in Turin.

The Nightlife Buzz

As the sun sets, Quadrilatero Romano transforms into one of Turin's liveliest nightlife hubs. The area's mix of historic charm and modern vibrancy creates a unique atmosphere that draws both locals and visitors.

Via Barbaroux is a popular street for nightlife, lined with a variety of bars and clubs. Caffè Al Bicerin at Piazza della Consolata 5 is a historic café that has been serving its signature bicerin (a layered coffee and chocolate drink) since

1763. It's a perfect spot for a cozy evening drink while soaking in the café's classic ambiance.

For a more contemporary experience, head to Mambo at Via delle Orfane 11. This trendy bar and club offers a dynamic atmosphere with live music, DJ sets, and a diverse selection of cocktails. The space is known for its stylish décor and energetic vibe, making it a favorite among Turin's young and hip crowd.

If you're looking for a more relaxed evening, La Drogheria at Via della Rocca 9 is a charming bar with a laid-back atmosphere. Housed in an old pharmacy, this unique venue serves an array of creative cocktails and provides a cozy setting for unwinding after a day of exploration.

Shopping and Exploring

Quadrilatero Romano is also a fantastic destination for shopping, offering a blend of high-end boutiques, vintage stores, and artisanal shops. Via dei Mille is home to several chic boutiques, including Galleria Luigi Tiepolo, where you can find unique fashion pieces and designer items.

For those with an interest in antiques, Antichità Baravalle at Via della Basilica 6 is a gem. This antique shop offers a range of period furniture, artwork, and curiosities, providing a glimpse into the past with every item.

Hidden Gems

One of the neighborhood's hidden gems is Borgo Medievale, a reconstructed medieval village located within the Valentino Park. Although technically just outside Quadrilatero Romano, it's worth a visit for its picturesque setting and historical architecture. The village, complete with a castle and charming streets, offers a tranquil escape from the city's hustle and bustle.

Piazza delle Erbe is another lesser-known spot that's worth exploring. This small square hosts a weekly market where you can find fresh produce, local crafts, and delicious street food. It's a great place to experience local life and pick up some unique souvenirs.

Practical Information

Getting There: Quadrilatero Romano is easily accessible by public transport. The Porta Nuova and Porta Susa train stations are within walking distance, and several bus and tram lines serve the area. The nearest metro stop is Re Umberto, just a short walk away.

Where to Stay: For a comfortable and stylish stay, consider the Hotel NH Collection Torino Piazza Carlina at Piazza Carlo Emanuele II 15. This boutique hotel is centrally located and offers modern amenities in a historic setting. Another excellent option is the Hotel Torino Palace at Corso Vittorio Emanuele II 54, known for its luxurious rooms and impeccable service.

Chapter 6: Day Trips from Turin

The Royal Residences of Piedmont: Palazzos and Gardens Fit for Royalty

1. The Royal Palace of Turin (Palazzo Reale)

Address: Piazza Castello, 10122 Torino TO, Italy

Website:Royal Palace of Turin

At the heart of Turin, the Royal Palace of Turin stands as a testament to the city's rich royal heritage. Originally constructed in the 16th century for the Duke of Savoy, this grand palace has been expanded and renovated over the centuries to become the primary residence of the Savoy family.

Architectural Highlights:

The palace showcases a mix of Baroque and Rococo styles, with lavish interiors that reflect the grandeur of the Savoy dynasty. The majestic Hall of Mirrors, adorned with opulent chandeliers and intricate frescoes, is particularly noteworthy. The Royal Apartments offer a glimpse into the luxurious lifestyle of the royal family, featuring beautifully decorated rooms with period furniture, tapestries, and artwork.

Gardens:

The palace is surrounded by formal gardens that once served as the royal family's private retreat. The manicured lawns, classical fountains, and elegant statues offer a serene escape within the bustling city. Don't miss the beautiful Parterre, a geometric garden design that exemplifies the Italian Renaissance approach to landscaping.

Tips for Visiting:

Hours: Open Tuesday to Sunday, 9:00 AM – 7:00 PM. Closed on Mondays.

Tickets: Purchase tickets in advance online to avoid long lines.

Guided Tours: Audio guides are available in multiple languages, but guided tours offer deeper insights into the palace's history.

2. The Palazzina di Caccia di Stupinigi

Address: Piazza Principe Amedeo, 7, 10042 Stupinigi TO, Italy

Website:Palazzina di Caccia

Located just a short drive from Turin, the Palazzina di Caccia di Stupinigi is a magnificent hunting lodge that exemplifies the Rococo style. Designed by the architect Filippo Juvarra, this palace was built in the early 18th century as a hunting retreat for the Savoy family.

Architectural Highlights:

The Palazzina di Caccia is renowned for its stunning facade, characterized by its grand symmetry and intricate detailing. The interior boasts lavish rooms decorated with frescoes, gilded moldings, and exquisite furniture. The grand hall, or Salone degli Stucchi, is a highlight with its opulent stucco work and elegant design.

Gardens:

The expansive park surrounding the palazzina features formal gardens and woodlands, designed to complement the palace's grandeur. The landscape includes manicured lawns, charming pathways, and picturesque ponds that offer a tranquil setting for leisurely strolls.

Tips for Visiting:

Hours: Open Tuesday to Sunday, 9:00 AM – 6:00 PM. Closed on Mondays.

Tickets: Tickets can be purchased at the entrance or online.

Guided Tours: Available in several languages, providing detailed historical context and architectural insights.

3. The Reggia di Venaria Reale

Address: Piazza della Repubblica, 4, 10078 Venaria Reale TO, Italy

Website:Reggia di Venaria Reale

Often referred to as the "Versailles of Italy," the Reggia di Venaria Reale is a stunning example of Baroque architecture and garden design. Located about 10 kilometers from Turin, this vast estate was once a royal hunting lodge and has been meticulously restored to its former glory.

Architectural Highlights:

The Reggia features a grandiose facade and an expansive interior that includes the magnificent Hall of Diana, adorned with intricate frescoes and chandeliers. The royal apartments, decorated with luxurious furnishings and artworks, provide a glimpse into the opulent lifestyle of the Savoy family.

Gardens:

The gardens of the Reggia di Venaria are a masterpiece of landscape design, featuring a blend of formal gardens, water features, and expansive lawns. The Grande Parterre, with its geometric patterns and intricate design, is particularly impressive. The gardens also include a botanical area and a maze, offering a delightful exploration experience.

Tips for Visiting:

Hours: Open Tuesday to Sunday, 9:00 AM – 7:00 PM. Closed on Mondays.

Tickets: Tickets can be purchased at the entrance or online. Combination tickets for the palace and gardens are available.

Guided Tours: Audio guides and guided tours are available to enrich your visit with historical and artistic insights.

4. The Castle of Rivoli (Castello di Rivoli)

Address: Piazza Mafalda di Savoia, 1, 10098 Rivoli TO, Italy

Website:Castle of Rivoli

Perched on a hill overlooking the city of Turin, the Castle of Rivoli is a historic fortress that has been transformed into a contemporary art museum. Originally built in the 9th century, it was later expanded and renovated by the Savoy family.

Architectural Highlights:

The castle's architecture blends medieval fortifications with Baroque enhancements. Inside, visitors can explore the museum's impressive collection of modern and contemporary art, set against the backdrop of the castle's historic interiors. The castle's various rooms and halls are adorned with both historical and modern art pieces.

Gardens:

The castle grounds include beautifully landscaped gardens that offer panoramic views of the surrounding Piedmont countryside. The formal gardens are designed with a blend of historical and contemporary elements, providing a scenic and peaceful retreat.

Tips for Visiting:

Hours: Open Tuesday to Sunday, 10:00 AM – 7:00 PM. Closed on Mondays.

Tickets: Purchase tickets at the entrance or online.

Guided Tours: Available in multiple languages, offering insights into both the castle's history and its contemporary art collection.

Sacra di San Michele: The Stunning Abbey on the Mountaintop

History and Significance

The Sacra di San Michele, or the Abbey of Saint Michael, dates back to the 10th century, with its origins believed to be rooted in a monastery founded by Benedictine monks. Its strategic location atop Mount Pirchiriano was chosen not only for its commanding views but also for its spiritual symbolism. The abbey was dedicated to Saint Michael the Archangel, a figure representing protection and guidance, making it a fitting site for a place of worship.

During the 11th and 12th centuries, the abbey flourished as a major pilgrimage site on the Via Francigena, the ancient route that connected northern Europe with Rome. The abbey's significance grew as it became a center of religious and cultural life in the region, attracting monks, pilgrims, and artists.

The abbey's history is marked by periods of grandeur and decline. It was sacked by Frederick Barbarossa in 1164, leading to its partial destruction. However, it was later rebuilt and has continued to stand as a testament to medieval architecture and resilience.

Architectural Marvel

The architecture of Sacra di San Michele is a stunning example of Romanesque and Gothic styles, showcasing the ingenuity and craftsmanship of the medieval builders. The abbey is divided into several sections, each with its unique architectural features.

The Gateway: The journey begins at the abbey's main entrance, which is an imposing gate flanked by two towers. The gateway is adorned with intricate carvings and sculptures, including representations of saints and biblical figures. As you walk through this gate, you are stepping into a realm of historical and spiritual significance.

The Cloister: Entering the abbey, you'll find yourself in the serene cloister, a peaceful courtyard surrounded by arcades. This area was used by the monks for meditation and reflection. The cloister's Romanesque columns and arches create a tranquil atmosphere, providing a stark contrast to the grandeur of the abbey's external architecture.

The Church: The abbey's church is the heart of the complex, featuring a magnificent nave and a series of chapels. The church's interior is adorned with beautiful frescoes and stained glass windows that depict various saints and biblical scenes. The high vaulted ceilings and intricate stonework add to the church's awe-inspiring presence.

The Crypt: Beneath the church lies the crypt, a dimly lit area with a series of ancient tombs and relics. The crypt is where many of the abbey's early monks were buried, and it offers a sense of historical depth and reverence.

The Tower: One of the most striking features of the abbey is its tall, cylindrical tower. This tower not only serves as a defensive structure but also provides a panoramic view of the surrounding landscape. Climbing to the top of the tower rewards you with an unobstructed vista of the valleys and peaks that stretch out before you.

Visiting the Abbey

Reaching Sacra di San Michele is an adventure in itself. The abbey is located approximately 40 kilometers (25 miles) from Turin, making it a convenient day trip from the city. The drive to the abbey takes you through picturesque landscapes, winding roads, and charming villages.

Address: Sacra di San Michele, 10050 Sant'Ambrogio di Torino, Turin, Italy

Getting There:

By Car: The most straightforward way to reach the abbey is by car. From Turin, take the A32 motorway towards Susa. Exit at Sant'Ambrogio and follow the signs to Sacra di San Michele. Parking is available at the base of the mountain, from where a short walk or shuttle bus will take you to the abbey.

By Train: For those using public transportation, take a train from Turin to Sant'Ambrogio di Torino. From the train station, you can either take a local bus or a taxi to reach the abbey's base.

By Foot: For the more adventurous, there are hiking trails that lead up to the abbey. These trails offer a rewarding experience, with beautiful views of the surrounding countryside.

Opening Hours: Sacra di San Michele is typically open daily from 9:00 AM to 6:00 PM. However, it's always a good idea to check the official website or contact the abbey directly for the most up-to-date information on opening hours and any potential closures.

Admission Fees: Entry to the abbey is usually free, but there may be a nominal fee for guided tours or access to certain areas. Guided tours are available and provide valuable insights into the abbey's history and architecture.

Tips for Visitors

Wear Comfortable Shoes: The terrain around the abbey can be uneven and steep, so it's essential to wear sturdy and comfortable footwear, especially if you're planning to explore the hiking trails.

Bring a Camera: The views from Sacra di San Michele are truly spectacular, and the abbey's architectural details are worth capturing. Don't forget to bring a camera to document your visit.

Respect the Sacred Space: Remember that Sacra di San Michele is a place of worship and historical significance. Be respectful of the surroundings and follow any guidelines provided by the abbey staff.

Check for Events: The abbey occasionally hosts special events, concerts, and exhibitions. Check the official website or local event listings to see if there are any interesting activities during your visit.

Local Attractions

While visiting Sacra di San Michele, consider exploring the surrounding area. The nearby town of Sant'Ambrogio di

Torino is charming and offers additional historical and cultural attractions. The Susa Valley, with its stunning landscapes and quaint villages, is also worth exploring.

Barolo and Langhe Wine Regions: Sipping the World's Finest Wines

A Journey to Barolo

Barolo, often referred to as the "King of Wines," is a small but influential village located at the heart of the Langhe region. Known for its robust Nebbiolo-based wines, Barolo has earned a prestigious reputation in the global wine community. The journey to Barolo from Turin takes about an hour and a half by car, and the scenic drive through vineyards and rolling hills is a treat in itself.

Barolo Wine Experience

One of the most immersive ways to experience Barolo is to visit the wine estates and cellars that dot the landscape. Many of these estates offer tours and tastings, providing an intimate look at the winemaking process and the chance to sample some of the region's finest offerings.

1. Marchesi di Barolo

Address: Via Vittorio Emanuele, 10, 12060 Barolo CN, Italy

Phone: +39 0173 56105

Marchesi di Barolo is one of the most historic and renowned wineries in the region. Founded in the 19th century, this estate combines tradition with modern winemaking techniques. The winery offers guided tours of its cellars, where you can learn about the aging process of Barolo wines, followed by a tasting of their flagship wines. The estate's tasting room provides a panoramic view of the vineyards, enhancing the overall experience.

2. Castello di Barolo

Address: Piazza Falletti, 1, 12060 Barolo CN, Italy

Phone: +39 0173 56216

Housed in a historic castle, Castello di Barolo provides a unique setting for wine tasting. The castle's historical and architectural significance adds depth to the tasting experience. The estate offers a variety of tasting options, including a selection of their prestigious Barolos and other local wines. The guided tours also include a visit to the wine museum within the castle, where you can delve into the history of Barolo wine.

3. Azienda Agricola Renato Ratti

Address: Via S. Giovanni, 8, 12060 La Morra CN, Italy

Phone: +39 0173 50155

Renato Ratti is known for its commitment to quality and innovation in winemaking. The estate provides a comprehensive tour that covers the vineyards, production areas, and aging cellars. Their tastings are highly regarded, and you can sample a range of their Barolo wines, including some from rare vintages. The estate's modern facilities and scenic location make for a memorable visit.

Discovering the Langhe Region

The Langhe region, encompassing Barolo, Barbaresco, and other nearby villages, is a UNESCO World Heritage site known for its stunning landscapes and exceptional wines. The rolling hills and lush vineyards create a picturesque backdrop for wine enthusiasts to explore.

Wine Tasting Tours

In addition to visiting individual estates, there are numerous wine tours available that offer a curated experience of the Langhe region. These tours often include transportation, guided visits to multiple wineries, and tastings, providing a convenient way to explore the area without the hassle of navigating on your own.

1. Langhe and Roero Wine Tours

Website: langheandroero.com

Phone: +39 0173 288008

Langhe and Roero Wine Tours offers a range of personalized tours that cater to different interests and preferences. Their tours often include visits to several renowned wineries, where you can taste a variety of wines and learn about the winemaking process. The company also arranges for local lunch stops, allowing you to pair your wine tastings with regional cuisine.

2. Gourmet Langhe

Website: gourmetlanghe.com

Phone: +39 0173 242453

Gourmet Langhe specializes in high-end wine tours and culinary experiences. Their tours often include visits to exclusive wineries, private tastings, and gourmet lunches or dinners featuring local specialties. This is a great option if you're looking for a more luxurious and personalized wine tasting experience.

Regional Highlights and Experiences

Aside from wine tasting, the Langhe region offers a variety of other experiences that complement your visit.

1. Trattoria della Storia

Address: Via Cavour, 23, 12060 Barolo CN, Italy

Phone: +39 0173 56275

For an authentic taste of local cuisine, Trattoria della Storia in Barolo is a must-visit. This charming restaurant offers a menu that features traditional Piedmontese dishes, including hearty risottos and rich meat dishes that pair perfectly with Barolo wine. The restaurant's warm atmosphere and attentive service make it a great place to enjoy a leisurely meal.

2. La Morra Panoramic Viewpoint

Address: Via Roma, 12, 12064 La Morra CN, Italy

For breathtaking views of the Langhe region, head to the panoramic viewpoint in La Morra. This spot offers sweeping vistas of the rolling hills and vineyards, providing a stunning backdrop for your wine country adventure. It's a perfect place to take a break and soak in the natural beauty of the region.

3. Barolo Wine Museum

Address: Piazza Falletti, 1, 12060 Barolo CN, Italy

Phone: +39 0173 56216

The Barolo Wine Museum, located in the Castello di Barolo, is a fascinating destination for wine lovers. The museum provides an in-depth look at the history and culture of Barolo wine, featuring exhibits on winemaking techniques, historical artifacts, and interactive displays. It's a great complement to your visits to local wineries.

Practical Tips for Your Visit

Transportation: While the Langhe region is easily accessible by car from Turin, consider hiring a driver or joining a guided tour if you plan on visiting multiple wineries. This ensures a relaxed experience without the worry of navigating unfamiliar roads.

Reservations: Many wineries and tours require advance reservations, especially during peak tourist seasons. Be sure to book your visits ahead of time to secure your preferred dates and times.

Dress Code: While there is no strict dress code for winery visits, smart casual attire is recommended. Comfortable shoes are also a must, as some tours involve walking through vineyards and production areas.

Language: While many wineries and tour guides speak English, learning a few basic Italian phrases can enhance your experience and show respect for the local culture.

Chapter 7: Practical Information

Getting Around Turin: Public Transport, Walking Routes, and Bike Rentals

Public Transport

Turin boasts an efficient and extensive public transportation system, comprising buses, trams, and a metro line. It's well-integrated, reliable, and a great way to explore the city's many neighborhoods and attractions.

Metro

Turin's metro system is modern and user-friendly, making it an excellent option for travelers looking to cover longer distances quickly. The metro consists of a single line (Line 1) that runs from the northern suburb of Sassi to the southern area of Lingotto. Key stops include:

Porta Nuova: This central hub is ideal for connections to main train stations and major attractions like the Museo Egizio.

Piazza Castello: Located near the Royal Palace, this stop places you in the heart of Turin's historic center.

Lingotto: This stop is convenient for reaching the modern conference center and shopping complex.

Metro trains run every 4-7 minutes from 5:30 AM to 11:30 PM, with services extending to midnight on Fridays and Saturdays.

Ticket Information: Tickets for the metro can be purchased at vending machines in metro stations or at tobacco shops. A standard ticket costs €1.70 and is valid for 90 minutes across all public transport modes within the urban area. For longer stays, consider a Torino + Piemonte Card, which offers unlimited travel for a set number of days.

Buses and Trams

Turin's bus and tram network complements the metro, covering areas not served by the underground. The trams, with their charming vintage design, provide a scenic way to travel.

Tram Line 4: Runs through the historic center, linking the Porta Nuova station to the historic district of Borgo Dora. It's ideal for sightseeing along the way.

Bus Line 55: Connects the University area with the bustling neighborhood of San Salvario, perfect for those exploring Turin's vibrant nightlife.

Trams and buses operate from 5:00 AM to 11:00 PM, with extended hours on weekends. Buses and trams run every 10-15 minutes during peak hours.

Ticket Information: Tickets for buses and trams are the same as those for the metro. They can be purchased from vending machines, newsstands, or directly from the driver. The same Torino + Piemonte Card also applies for unlimited travel.

Taxi Services

For more personalized transportation, taxis are readily available throughout Turin. You'll find taxi stands at major squares and transport hubs like Porta Nuova and Piazza Castello. Alternatively, you can call a taxi or use ride-hailing apps like MyTaxi (now Free Now) and Uber.

Fares: The base fare for a taxi is around €3.50, with additional charges based on distance and time of day. The rates are regulated and visible inside the taxi.

Walking Routes

Turin is a city best explored on foot, especially in its historic center. The compact and walkable layout means you can easily cover many of the city's highlights without needing public transport.

Key Walking Routes

Historic Center Walk

Start at Piazza Castello: Admire the Royal Palace and the Cathedral of Saint John the Baptist.

Stroll along Via Roma: Enjoy high-end shopping and grand architecture.

Head to Piazza San Carlo: Often referred to as the "Living Room of Turin," this square is surrounded by elegant cafés and baroque buildings.

Art and Culture Trail

Begin at Mole Antonelliana: Tour the National Cinema Museum and enjoy panoramic views from the top.

Walk to Museo Egizio: Explore one of the world's most significant Egyptian collections.

End at Piazza Vittorio Veneto: Relax at a café with views of the Po River and the surrounding hills.

Po River Walk

Start at Ponte Vittorio Emanuele I: Enjoy a scenic walk along the riverbank.

Explore Borgo Medievale: A charming medieval village and castle on the river's edge.

Continue to Parco del Valentino: Stroll through this expansive park and its picturesque gardens.

Tips for Walking

Comfortable Shoes: Turin's cobblestone streets can be uneven, so wear comfortable walking shoes.

Map: Use a map or a navigation app to help with directions. Many historical sites are well-signposted.

Weather: Turin's weather can be unpredictable. Dress in layers and carry an umbrella, especially in the spring and fall.

Bike Rentals

Cycling is a fantastic way to see Turin, especially with its growing network of bike lanes and paths. The city offers several options for bike rentals, catering to both casual riders and serious cyclists.

Bike Sharing Programs

TOBike: Turin's official bike-sharing service allows you to rent bikes from various stations around the city. Bikes can be rented by the hour or day and returned to any TOBike station.

How to Rent: Register online or at a TOBike station. You can use a credit card or a smartphone app for payment.

Costs: The first 30 minutes are usually free, with additional charges of around €1.50 per additional 30 minutes.

Bike Rental Shops

Bike Rental Torino

Address: Via della Rocca, 9, 10123 Torino TO

Details: Offers a range of bikes including city bikes, e-bikes, and mountain bikes. Daily and weekly rates available.

Contact: +39 011 813 5638

Rent a Bike Torino

Address: Corso Vittorio Emanuele II, 79, 10121 Torino TO

Details: Provides various rental options, including guided bike tours of Turin.

Contact: +39 011 817 7117

Cycling Routes

Along the Po River: This flat, scenic route follows the riverbanks and is perfect for a leisurely ride.

To the Hill of Superga: For the more adventurous, cycling up to the Basilica of Superga offers a rewarding view of the city and surrounding landscape.

Tips for Cycling

Safety: Always wear a helmet and use bike lights if riding after dark.

Bike Lanes: Stick to designated bike lanes where available.

Bike Repair: Many rental shops offer basic bike repair services or advice on where to find repairs.

Where to Stay: Accommodation for Every Budget

Luxury Stays: Indulgence in Style

1. Principi di Piemonte

Address: Via Giuseppe Mazzini, 11, 10123 Torino TO, Italy

A beacon of luxury in the heart of Turin, the Principi di Piemonte epitomizes elegance and sophistication. Located just steps from Piazza Castello, this five-star hotel offers opulent rooms adorned with classic decor and modern amenities. Guests can enjoy a panoramic view of the city from the rooftop terrace, dine at the renowned restaurant, or unwind in the wellness center, which includes a fitness room and a sauna. The hotel's concierge service is impeccable, ensuring personalized recommendations and arrangements for a truly memorable stay.

Tip: Book a suite to experience the full splendor of this historic hotel's grandeur. Early booking often secures better rates and room preferences.

2. Grand Hotel Sitea

Address: Via Carlo Alberto, 35, 10123 Torino TO, Italy

Situated near the elegant Via Roma and Piazza San Carlo, the Grand Hotel Sitea combines classic charm with modern comfort. This five-star establishment boasts spacious rooms, high ceilings, and luxurious furnishings. The hotel is renowned for its impeccable service and fine dining at its in-house restaurant, which offers a selection of exquisite Italian dishes. For those looking to explore Turin's cultural treasures, the hotel's central location provides easy access to key landmarks and shopping districts.

Tip: The hotel often features special packages that include guided city tours or spa treatments, adding extra value to your stay.

Mid-Range Comfort: Style and Value

3. Hotel Turin Palace

Address: Piazza Garelli, 1, 10138 Torino TO, Italy

Located near Porta Nuova Train Station, Hotel Turin Palace is a stylish mid-range option that offers both comfort and convenience. The hotel features modern rooms with tasteful decor, complimentary Wi-Fi, and a well-equipped fitness center. Guests can enjoy a generous buffet breakfast each morning and relax in the elegant lounge area. Its proximity to public transport makes it an excellent base for exploring the city's attractions and dining options.

Tip: Consider booking a room with a city view to enjoy a picturesque panorama of Turin's skyline.

4. NH Collection Torino Piazza Carlina

Address: Piazza Carlo Emanuele II, 15, 10123 Torino TO, Italy

The NH Collection Torino Piazza Carlina is set in a beautifully restored 17th-century palace, offering a blend of historical charm and modern luxury. The hotel's spacious rooms come with contemporary amenities, and the breakfast buffet is renowned for its quality. The on-site restaurant serves a range of Italian and international dishes. The hotel's location on Piazza Carlo Emanuele II provides easy access to nearby attractions and the vibrant nightlife of the Quadrilatero Romano.

Tip: The hotel often provides seasonal promotions and special rates for early bookings.

Budget-Friendly Options: Comfort and Affordability

5. Hotel Victoria

Address: Via Nino Bixio, 4, 10123 Torino TO, Italy

Hotel Victoria offers a comfortable and affordable stay without compromising on quality. Located a short walk from Piazza Castello, this three-star hotel provides clean, cozy rooms with basic amenities and free Wi-Fi. The hotel features a simple but pleasant breakfast room and offers a range of Italian and continental options. Its central location allows for easy access to Turin's main attractions, making it an excellent choice for budget-conscious travelers.

Tip: Check for any special deals or promotions, especially during off-peak seasons, to get the best value for your money.

6. Hotel Dock Milano

Address: Via Cernaia, 46, 10122 Torino TO, Italy

A short distance from the Porta Susa Train Station, Hotel Dock Milano is an excellent budget choice that doesn't skimp on comfort. The hotel offers clean, functional rooms with essential amenities, including free Wi-Fi and a complimentary breakfast. Its convenient location makes it easy to access public transport and explore nearby attractions. The hotel's friendly staff and affordable rates make it a popular choice among both leisure and business travelers.

Tip: Booking in advance can secure better rates and room availability, especially during peak travel seasons.

Hostels and Alternative Stays: Social and Economical

7. OstellOlinda

Address: Via P. Maroncelli, 23, 10156 Torino TO, Italy

For travelers seeking a more communal and budget-friendly option, OstellOlinda provides a unique hostel experience in Turin. Located in a vibrant neighborhood, this hostel offers dormitory-style accommodations as well as private rooms. It features a relaxed atmosphere, a communal kitchen, and organized social events. The hostel's proximity to public transport makes it easy to explore the city, while its affordable rates cater to budget travelers and backpackers.

Tip: Booking a private room can offer a bit more privacy while still enjoying the hostel's social atmosphere.

8. Torino Sweet Home

Address: Various locations throughout Turin

Torino Sweet Home offers a range of vacation rentals and self-catering apartments throughout Turin. This option provides flexibility and a homely atmosphere, ideal for families or groups. The apartments are well-equipped with kitchen facilities, allowing guests to prepare their own meals. With properties scattered across the city, you can choose a location that best suits your itinerary and preferences.

Tip: Check the reviews and ratings of individual apartments to ensure a good fit for your needs and expectations.

Insider Tips and Safety Advice: Navigating Turin Like a Pro

Getting Around Turin

1. Public Transport: Navigating with Ease

Turin's public transport system is efficient and well-connected, making it easy to explore the city. The key components are buses, trams, and the Metro.

Metro: The Turin Metro has a single line, Line 1, running from the northern suburb of S. Giovanni to the southern end of Lingotto. It's a quick and straightforward way to traverse the city center. Tickets can be purchased at vending machines located in metro stations or through the GTT (Gruppo Torinese Trasporti) app.

Buses and Trams: The city's extensive network of buses and trams covers areas not served by the metro. For example, Tram 4 takes you to the picturesque district of San Salvario, while Bus 61 connects the city center to the charming hills of the Collina Torinese. Tickets are valid on all forms of public transportation and should be validated before boarding.

Tip: Consider purchasing a Torino + Piemonte Card for unlimited travel on public transport, along with discounts on various attractions.

2. Biking and Walking: Embrace Turin's Pedestrian-Friendly Streets

Turin is a bike-friendly city with numerous bike lanes and paths. Bike-sharing services like ToBike make it easy to rent a bike for a few hours or the entire day. The city's flat terrain and beautiful architecture make biking and walking enjoyable ways to explore.

Bike-Friendly Areas: The Po River banks and the Valentino Park are ideal spots for a leisurely bike ride or walk.

Walking: The historic center is best explored on foot. Stroll along Via Roma and Piazza San Carlo to soak in Turin's elegant atmosphere, and don't miss the charming, narrow streets of the Quadrilatero Romano for an authentic local experience.

3. Taxis and Ride-Sharing: Convenient Alternatives

Taxis are readily available throughout Turin, and you can hail one from the street or book one through the Taxi Torino app. Ride-sharing services like Uber are also operational, providing an alternative for those who prefer private transport.

Insider Tips for Exploring Turin

1. Discovering Hidden Gems

While Turin's major landmarks are impressive, the city's true character shines through its lesser-known spots.

The Balon Market: Held every Saturday in the Borgo Dora district, this vibrant flea market is a treasure trove of antiques, vintage clothing, and unique collectibles. For a true local experience, visit the market early in the morning.

Address: Piazza della Repubblica, 10122 Torino

Borgo Medievale: Located in Valentino Park, this reconstructed medieval village offers a whimsical glimpse into the past with its quaint architecture and artisan shops. It's a perfect spot for a leisurely afternoon.

Address: Viale Virgilio, 10126 Torino

Caffè Al Bicerin: Founded in 1763, this historic café is renowned for its namesake drink, a rich blend of espresso, chocolate, and cream. It's a must-visit for coffee aficionados.

Address: Piazza della Consolata, 5, 10122 Torino

2. Engaging with Locals

Turinians are known for their friendliness. Engaging with locals can enrich your experience and offer insights into hidden gems and local customs.

Language: While many people speak English, learning a few basic Italian phrases can go a long way. Greetings like "Buongiorno" (Good morning) and "Grazie" (Thank you) are appreciated.

Dining Etiquette: When dining, it's customary to greet the staff and say "Buon appetito" before starting your meal. In restaurants, it's common to leave a small tip, around 5-10% of the bill.

Safety Advice: Navigating Turin with Confidence

1. General Safety Tips

Turin is generally a safe city, but it's wise to stay vigilant, especially in crowded areas.

Pickpocketing: Like many tourist destinations, pickpocketing can be a concern, particularly in busy areas such as the central markets or on public transportation. Keep your belongings secure and be mindful of your surroundings.

Emergency Numbers: Familiarize yourself with local emergency numbers. For police assistance, dial 113; for medical emergencies, dial 118.

2. Health and Safety

Health Care: If you need medical assistance, Turin has several reputable hospitals and clinics. The Ospedale Molinette and Ospedale Sant'Anna are two major hospitals in the city.

Ospedale Molinette: Corso Bramante, 88, 10126 Torino

Ospedale Sant'Anna: Corso Cavallotti, 26, 10128 Torino

Water Quality: The tap water in Turin is safe to drink. However, if you prefer bottled water, it's readily available in supermarkets and convenience stores.

3. Navigating Turin's Nightlife

Safe Areas: Turin's nightlife is vibrant, particularly in the San Salvario and Quadrilatero Romano districts. These areas are generally safe, but it's wise to stick to well-lit streets and avoid walking alone late at night.

Transportation After Hours: If you're out late, consider using public transport or a taxi to get back to your accommodation.

The Metro runs until around midnight, and taxis are available throughout the night.

Practical Advice

1. Currency and Payments

Currency: The local currency is the Euro (€). Credit and debit cards are widely accepted, but it's a good idea to carry some cash for smaller establishments or markets.

ATMs: ATMs are widely available throughout the city. Look for machines in well-lit, secure areas.

2. Shopping and Souvenirs

Local Specialties: Turin is famous for its chocolate, particularly the gianduiotto. Visit local chocolate shops like Piazza San Carlo 174 for high-quality souvenirs.

Shopping Districts: For a mix of high-end and boutique shopping, head to Via Roma and Via Po. These streets offer a range of stores from luxury brands to unique Italian finds.

Conclusion

As you prepare to bid farewell to Turin, you leave behind a city that has likely charmed and captivated you with its elegance, history, and vibrant culture. Turin, with its regal architecture, world-renowned museums, and delightful culinary scene, is a destination that offers much more than meets the eye. From the grandeur of the Royal Palace to the tranquil beauty of Valentino Park, Turin is a city that invites exploration and discovery.

Your time in Turin has undoubtedly been filled with moments of awe and wonder, whether you were marveling at the Egyptian treasures in the Museo Egizio, savoring a decadent gianduiotto in a historic café, or wandering through the lively streets of the Quadrilatero Romano. This guide has aimed to be your compass, providing you with insider tips, practical advice, and a deep dive into the city's unique character.

Turin's allure lies not only in its grandiose landmarks and historical significance but also in the everyday experiences that make it a living, breathing city. Whether it was engaging with locals over a coffee, discovering hidden markets, or simply soaking in the ambiance of a quiet piazza, these moments are the essence of what makes Turin special. As you reflect on your journey, take with you the stories and memories of a city that blends tradition with modernity, grandeur with intimacy.

Your adventure in Turin doesn't have to end with your departure. The experiences you've had and the discoveries you've made will continue to inspire and enrich your understanding of Italy. Perhaps you'll find yourself reminiscing about a stroll along the Po River or the delightful flavors of local cuisine. Turin has a way of leaving a lasting impression, and its charm often lingers long after you've returned home.

If you've enjoyed your time in Turin, consider staying connected with the city through various channels. Follow local events, discover new cultural happenings, and keep an eye on updates from Turin's vibrant arts and culinary scenes. Turin is a city that continually evolves, and staying connected allows you to be a part of its ongoing story.

As you conclude your journey with this guide, we hope you feel enriched by the depth and diversity of Turin. This city, often overlooked in favor of its more famous Italian counterparts, offers a unique and rewarding experience for those who take the time to explore its many facets.

Thank you for allowing this guide to accompany you on your adventure. Turin is a city that welcomes you with open arms, and we hope you've left with a newfound appreciation for its beauty and complexity. Until your next visit, may the memories of Turin's splendid landscapes, its rich history, and its warm, welcoming spirit continue to inspire and delight you.

Arrivederci, and safe travels on all your future journeys.

Printed in Great Britain
by Amazon